CRAFT LAB FOR KIDS

52 DIY PROJECTS TO INSPIRE, EXCITE, AND EMPOWER KIDS TO CREATE USEFUL, BEAUTIFUL HANDMADE GOODS

STEPHANIE CORFEE

QUARRY

CONTENTS

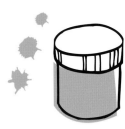

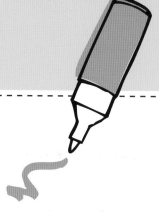

UNIT 5 CLASSIC CRAFTS WITH A TWIST

Tried-and-true crafts and games updated for kids today

UNIT 6 15-MINUTE MAKES

Quickie crafts you can make in a flash

UNIT 7 CRAFTING WITH KINDNESS

Thoughtful creations to brighten someone's day

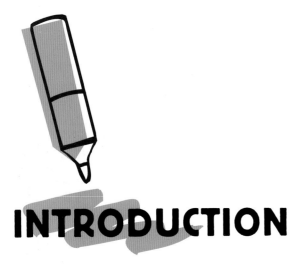

INTRODUCTION

Learn the basics of classic handicrafts with a twist, like wall weaving, embroidery (on canvas sneakers!), and God's Eyes. Be amazed by projects that seem almost like magic! Photo-Transfer Memory Boxes, Homemade Bath Bombs, and T-Shirt "Yarn" Braided Lanyards will delight and surprise.

This book provides a creative outlet for your body and soul. The "Crafting with Kindness" section will warm your heart as you use your hands. The section on self-care crafts focuses on projects that will relax your body and give you some "me time." And then, of course, there is a section titled "Kids Just Wanna Have Fun." This part of the book is made for a good time. Make Photo Backdrops for a party, Wonderful Wands, and even Travel Tic-Tac-Toe!

T-Shirt Tote Bags (page 112)

Artsy Desktop Dry Erase Board (page 114)

Want to be crafty with limited time? Try one of the 15-Minute Makes, such as T-Shirt Tote Bags, Artsy Desktop Dry Erase Boards, or Easy Fringed Leather Keyrings. Instant gratification can be fun sometimes! Then on a rainy day full of movies on the couch, you can tackle one of the lengthier projects in the book. The Homemade Rainbow Piñata, No-Sew Fringed Pet Blankets, and Mini Cross-Stitch Zipper Pulls are all perfect choices to work on for a whole afternoon.

So try your hand and challenge your abilities. You'll be amazed by what you can do and inspired to grow in your creativity.

Easy Fringed Leather Keyring (page 110)

ESSENTIAL TOOLS & MATERIALS

ARTS & CRAFTS STORE SUPPLIES

Craft paints, brushes, permanent markers, and paper are a good start when it comes to basic supplies. Add some extras like yarn, embroidery supplies, double-sided tape, glue sticks, decoupage medium, superglue, fabric dye, and pipe cleaners to expand your toolbox. Finally, you'll need a few more unique items from the crafts section, like shrink film, polymer clay, armature wire, and leather scraps to complete the projects in this book.

ITEMS TO UPCYCLE OR RECYCLE

Once you begin to craft, you will see the world with new eyes. Everything suddenly looks like a craft opportunity. So start saving things like old sweaters, jeans, and even shoes that are past their prime. You can give them a second life with a little creativity. Empty jars and bottles and worn leather goods like bags and belts can also be reimagined. Even found objects like pebbles, branches, and backyard leaves and flowers can turn into a fun craft if you just have the vision to see it.

Arts and crafts supplies

Items for upcycling
or recycling

KITCHEN AND HOUSEHOLD ITEMS

Lots of useful homemade projects start in the kitchen or household cupboards. You likely have many of the things you need already on hand. Keep an eye out for baking soda, white sugar, coconut oil, food coloring, and gelatin. Shaving cream and essential oils also come in handy. Office supplies like thumbtacks, paperclips, and a hole punch are all excellent for crafting too!

PROJECT-SPECIFIC SUPPLIES

Finally, there are specialized supplies required for a few of the projects in this book. It's not likely that jewelry findings, eye hooks, ¼-in. (6 mm) dowels, guitar picks, and citric acid are just sitting on the shelf in most closets. Take a look at the materials list for your project in advance to see if a trip to the store is needed before you begin.

PREPPING FOR SUCCESS

For kids: Before you begin a project, gather all the supplies you'll need and protect your workspace with newspaper or a drop cloth if necessary. It's far more enjoyable to complete a project without constantly running to fetch items you need as you go along. It's also much nicer to clean up afterward if your mess is contained.

For adults: If the project will be completed by multiple kids or kids of different ages, be sure to read instructions ahead of time and note the "Little Hands" adaptations included with some of the more complex projects. Many projects also include additional tips or suggestions to change, personalize, and modify the craft. With these extra instructions, almost anyone will be able to enjoy each project in their own way.

Kitchen and household items

Spruce Up Your Stuff

One great aspect of crafting is reimagining things we already own. Skip the store when you want something new! Instead, look around the house for items that only need a little facelift to be fabulous. Embellish some plain-Jane shoes. Turn blank notecards into showstoppers with paint marbling. Decoupage some glassware that was destined for the recycle bin. Once you've opened your eyes to the concept of reinvention and upcycling, you'll be excited to "treasure hunt" for items that need a makeover. No tattered bag or boring tee will be safe from your savvy creativity. You're the generation that champions sustainability and aims to create less waste in the world. It's a lesson worth sharing with everyone!

SECRET BOOK
HIDING SPOT

Upcycle an old and tattered book into a secret place to stash your stuff. Put your math and measuring skills to work to replace book pages with cardboard edges to conceal savings, special mementos, notes, or other cherished items. Once your project is complete, tuck it on the shelf amongst other books, and nobody will suspect a thing!

This project is best suited for older kids or younger kids who have help from an adult.

MATERIALS

☐ Old hardback book

☐ Ruler or tape measure

☐ Scissors or razor cutting tool

☐ Sturdy scrap cardboard
  (like from a clean pizza box)

☐ Pencil

☐ Hot glue gun

☐ Glue stick

☐ Felt

1. Measure the length from the bottom spine of the book all the way around to the top spine of the book to get a length measurement (fig. 1). Also measure the thickness of the book pages to get a width measurement. Write them down.

2. Use the edge of a pair of scissors or a razor cutting tool (with adult help) to cut the front and back book endpapers along the spine and release the book pages from the hard cover and spine (fig. 2).

3. Using the length and width measurements from step 1, cut two strips of cardboard (fig. 3). Add ½" (1 cm) to the width measurement before cutting. Keep the length the same. Once the strips are cut, measure and mark a pencil line ½" (1 cm) away from the long edge.

4. Press in with a sharp pencil or pen along the pencil line to score the cardboard strips. Crease the cardboard along the line to create a flat flange for gluing the strips to the book cover (fig. 4). Do this for both strips.

5. Hold the cardboard strip along the book edge. Mark the corner with pencil line (fig. 5). You will repeat this step for the top corner and second strip of cardboard as well.

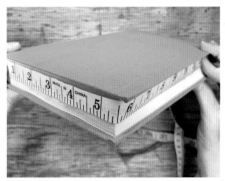

Fig. 1: Measure the book pages' length and width.

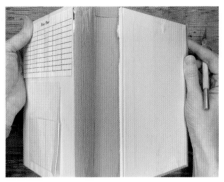

Fig. 2: Separate the cover from the book pages.

Fig. 3: Measure and cut the cardboard strips.

Fig. 4: Fold the cardboard strip.

Fig. 5: Mark the corners.

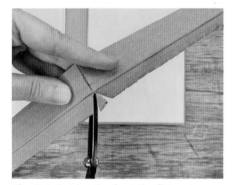

Fig. 6: Snip triangles from the flange to make corners.

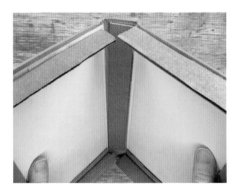

Fig. 7: Hot glue the cardboard walls to the book front and back.

Fig. 8: Add the felt lining.

6. Cut triangles out of the flange (the ½" [1 cm] segment of the strip) at each corner mark (fig. 6). This allows them to be folded to create the walls of the book box.

7. Use hot glue or another fast-hold adhesive to attach the cardboard walls to the front cover of the book, very close to the edge. Repeat to attach the cardboard walls to the back cover of the book. Attach this strip just a slight 1/16" (1.6 mm) or so further from the book edge than you did on the front cover (fig. 7).

8. Glue a piece of felt to the inside of your book box to conceal all cardboard edges and complete your hiding spot (fig. 8).

HAND-EMBROIDERED
CANVAS SNEAKERS

Turn boring or tattered canvas shoes into works of art with visible mending that is as beautiful as it is useful. This project uses very simple stitching patterns inspired by *sashiko*, which means "little stabs." Rows and rows of repetitive stitches in basic patterns are the hallmark of this technique, which is traditionally used to patch worn clothing in a way that is lovely to the eye. The more stitches, the better! Plentiful stitches equal a more dynamic and intricate finished masterpiece for your feet!

MATERIALS

☐ Fabric scraps

☐ Scissors

☐ Canvas shoes

☐ Fabric glue

☐ Embroidery needle

☐ Embroidery floss *(various colors)*

☐ Thimble *(optional)*

Teachable Moment

The *sashiko* stitching technique has been around for a long time. It was born out of necessity at a time when cloth was scarce and valued. It offers a beautiful way to conserve resources and save worn items rather than throw them away.

1. Cut shapes from fabric scraps and position them on the shoes as you would do with a paper collage (fig. 1).

2. Use fabric glue sparingly to tack the scraps into place before you begin stitching (fig. 2). Allow to dry. Note: Don't place any designs deep into the toe box of the shoe. It will be difficult to maneuver your needle in that small space.

Fig. 1: Arrange the fabric scraps.

Fig. 2: Glue down the scraps.

Fig. 3: Stitch the first colors and main design.

Fig. 4: Knot the floss tails.

Fig. 5: Add a new stitch color and design.

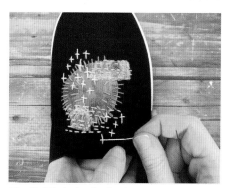

Fig. 6: Stitch the final color and design.

3. Create a stitch pattern that follows or accentuates the shape of one of your scrap patches (fig. 3). In this case, single stitches radiate outward all around the circle scrap. (Use a thimble if you have a hard time pushing the needle through the canvas.)

4. Knot the floss on the inside of the shoe each time you finish with a color (fig. 4). Trim the tails close to the knot.

5. Use a second color of floss to create a new stitch pattern across the scraps (fig. 5). In this case, rows of short stitches are overlapped across the fabric scraps, existing stitches, and shoe canvas.

6. Use a final stitch color and design (fig. 6). In this case, white floss is used to scatter little cross designs across the fabric scraps, existing stitches, and shoe canvas. The small crisscross designs are a popular choice that add lots of personality.

LITTLE HANDS

This project is definitely best for older kids, but little ones can still participate! Have them practice colorful stitches on scrap fabric and simply attach with fabric glue.

DECOUPAGE
BOTTLE VASE

You'll never look at a glass jar or bottle the same again once you see what they can become! A little colored tissue paper can transform bottles destined for the recycling bin into adorable, colorful vessels to hold flowers, pens, coins, and more. Keep on the lookout for patterned or foil-accented tissue papers to add into your project to get a real wow factor!

MATERIALS

☐ Glass jars and bottles (wide-mouth containers are the most versatile)

☐ Nonabrasive scrubbing sponge

☐ Colored and patterned tissue paper

☐ Scissors

☐ White glue or decoupage medium (if using glue, mix 3 parts glue with 1 part water)

☐ Paintbrush

1. Soak the glass vessels in a sink of warm, soapy water to help remove residue and loosen labels (fig. 1). Use a nonabrasive scrubbing sponge to tackle stubborn bits of label adhesive.

2. Cut tissue paper into strips or any shape you prefer (fig. 2).

3. Begin brushing decoupage medium onto the jar, starting at the bottom (fig. 3). This way, it will be dry enough to place on a table by the time you finish gluing. Work in small areas at a time to prevent the medium from drying before you get to it.

Fig. 1: Wash the glassware and remove any labels.

Fig. 2: Cut the tissue paper into strips.

Fig. 3: Brush the decoupage medium onto the jar.

Fig. 4: Layer on the tissue strips.

Fig. 5: Coat the tissue with more decoupage medium.

Fig. 6: Work the tissue into any crevices.

4. Add the tissue paper strips to the jar (fig. 4). Overlap them to create interesting texture and color blending that make the finished project so beautiful.

5. Alternate adding new strips and coating the strips already applied as you go (fig. 5). The idea is to glue the strips down *and* coat them with the medium thoroughly by the time the jar is complete.

6. The neck of your jar will likely have grooves that held the lid on. Use the side of the brush to gently coax the tissue into these areas with a generous amount of medium and a light hand so the tissue doesn't tear (fig. 6).

NOW TRY THIS!

Experiment with different color combinations! An ombré jar with navy tissue near the bottom, medium blue in the middle, and light blue at the top would be beautiful and beachy! Or try a rainbow. Cut circles from tissue paper and play with layering them on like confetti.

STENCILED AND STAMPED
GRAPHIC TEES

You can mimic the look and feel of a screen-printed tee with soft fabric paint and simple supplies. Try using blue painter's tape to create cool reversed graphics. Or try making homemade stamps with adhesive-back foam sheets from the craft store and scrap cardboard. Once you get started, you won't be able to stop!

MATERIALS

☐ Blank T-shirts

☐ Blue painter's tape

☐ Scissors

☐ Foam stamps or stencil brushes

☐ Soft fabric paint

☐ Adhesive foam sheets

☐ Corrugated cardboard

- One piece (approximately 10 × 12″ [25.5 × 30.5 cm]) to place inside the shirt while painting to prevent bleed through and give a firm surface for applying the paint

- One piece to cut up and use as backing for the homemade foam stamps

☐ Foam brush

Fig. 1: Make a painter's tape outline on the shirt.

Fig. 2: Cut shapes from the painter's tape.

Fig. 3: Complete your tape art and press down the tape edges firmly.

Fig. 4: Stamp paint inside the border.

Fig. 5: Remove the tape to reveal your design.

TAPE-STENCILED TEES

1. Tape off a shape on the T-shirt front (fig. 1) with painter's tape. You can try a square, star, or other simple design.

2. Cut shapes from the tape that will be masked out during the painting process and retain the color of your shirt (fig. 2).

3. Complete your cutout designs and place them inside the taped off border (fig. 3). Be sure that all the edges are pressed down well to avoid paint seeping under the tape.

4. Load a foam stamp with soft fabric paint and press the color onto the tee inside the border (fig. 4). Use a bouncing motion and do not rub the brush side to side, which may force paint under tape edges.

5. Once the paint is tacky/mostly dry, carefully lift off the masking tape to reveal your graphic (fig. 5)!

(continued)

NOW TRY THIS!

- Try the reverse stencil/masking technique without the taped border to achieve a more freestyle edge on your design.

- Cut letters from the foam sheets and spell out words on your tees!

STAMPED TEES

1. Cut a simple shape from an adhesive foam sheet and remove the backing (fig. 1).

2. Triple the thickness of the stamp shape by peeling and sticking it to more foam sheeting and trimming it close to the first shape (fig. 2).

3. Peel and stick the triple-thick foam shape to corrugated cardboard. Trim about ¼" (6 mm) away from the foam edges so there is a bit of room to grip (fig. 3).

4. Apply an even layer of soft fabric paint to the foam stamp using a foam brush (fig. 4).

5. Press the stamp firmly to the shirt and carefully peel it away to reveal your design (fig. 5). Repeat!

Hint: If you want to change colors using the same stamp, be sure to thoroughly blot the stamp and then gently wipe it so that none of the original color remains.

Fig. 1: Cut the foam sheet shape and peel off the backing.

Fig. 2: Peel, stick, and trim the foam shape to get a triple-thick foam shape.

Fig. 3: Stick the foam shape to cardboard and trim.

Fig. 4: Apply paint to the stamp with a foam brush.

Fig. 5: Stamp your shirt.

LITTLE HANDS

Random stamp placement is easier for little ones. Try making a simple stamp (try a chunky heart or lightning bolt) and let kids place and overlap different colors any way they choose.

FAUX EMBOSSED
LEATHER CUFF

This craft yields great results every time! The simplest tools and basic skills result in a super cool wearable craft you'll want to share with all your friends. It's a great activity for a rainy summer afternoon, or even as a party activity and favor since there is no mess and very few supplies. Don't throw away those drained ballpoint pens! Here's a use for them.

MATERIALS

☐ Pencil

☐ Vegetable tanned leather bracelet blanks

☐ Damp rag

☐ Empty ballpoint pen

☐ Brown marker (a small felt-tip marker is recommended)

☐ Leather conditioner or shoe polish (optional)

1. Use a pencil to lightly sketch your design on the leather (fig. 1).

2. Use a damp rag to go over the surface of the leather a few times to moisten and soften the surface to accept deeper embossing (fig. 2).

3. Use an empty ballpoint pen to trace over the sketched lines and create an indentation (fig. 3). Press lightly at first and go over the marks a few times. Press a bit harder as you go to make the designs deeper and deeper.

4. Use a brown marker to carefully fill the indented designs (fig. 4).

5. If you'd like, use leather shoe polish to stain the cuff, or use leather conditioner to shine up and protect your cuff (fig. 5).

Fig. 1: Sketch the design.

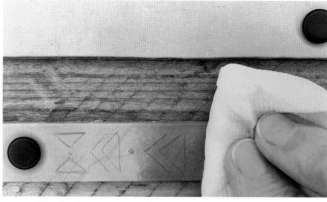

Fig. 2: Wet the leather with water.

Fig. 3: Create the embossed designs.

Fig. 4: Fill the designs with marker.

Fig. 5: Stain and seal the cuff.

NOW TRY THIS!

- Try this technique on thrifted leather goods like old belts or handbag straps with leather thick enough to make an indentation.

- Emboss the names of both you and your BFF onto two cuffs for a homemade set of friendship bracelets!

HANDMADE TASSELS

A tassel-making afternoon is always a great idea. Homemade tassels can be used in so many ways, and the process of making them is repetitive and relaxing. You can fill a whole box while watching a favorite movie or having a TV marathon. Make them from yarn, as shown here, or get creative with fabric scraps, string, leather cord, or even strips of tissue paper. Save them for pretty gift wrapping, decoration on handbags, zipper pulls, or party decor.

MATERIALS

☐ Cardboard

☐ Yarn

☐ Scissors

1. Cut a rectangle of cardboard about 4" (10 cm) wide, and the same length as you'd like your finished tassel. This example is about 5½" (14 cm) long. Cut out a notch as shown (fig. 1).

2. Cut a length of yarn about 8" (20 cm) and lay it across the top of the cardboard form. Starting at the bottom, wrap the rest of the yarn around and around the bit of yarn and the cardboard from bottom to top about 15 times (fig. 2). You can wrap more times for a fluffier tassel, if you like.

Fig. 1: Cut the cardboard forms.

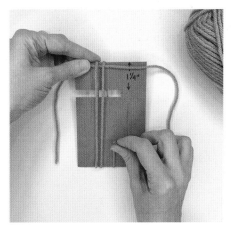

Fig. 2: Wrap the yarn bottom to top.

Fig. 3: Snip the yarn.

Fig. 4: Tie off the hanger.

Fig. 5: Tie off the tassel fringe.

Fig. 6: Trim the fringe.

3. Snip the yarn at the bottom of the cardboard so that both cut ends are at the bottom (fig. 3).

4. Tie a tight knot in the bit of string at the top of the cardboard and leave the tails (fig. 4). These will be used for attaching your tassel wherever you like.

5. Slip a length of yarn through the notch in the cardboard and tie. Wrap it around the neck of the tassel several times and tie off again (fig. 5). This secures the tassel fringe like cinching a dress at the waist.

6. Slide the yarn off the cardboard and cut the loop at the bottom open with scissors to create the fringe. Snip off any stray lengths to make it even (fig. 6).

PATCHWORK GUITAR OR UKULELE STRAP

Calling all musicians! Express yourself through your songs *and* your style with this patchwork strap cover for your guitar or ukulele. The simple design relies on a stretchy knit back so the cover can just slide on and off your current strap. Make a few different covers to suit your mood, outfit, or musical event.

MATERIALS

☐ Scissors

☐ Knit fabric

☐ Lightweight cotton woven fabric (like quilting fabric)

☐ Various scraps of cotton woven fabric for the patches

☐ Pinking shears *(optional)*

☐ Fusible bonding web tape

☐ Iron

☐ Embroidery floss *(various colors)*

☐ Embroidery needle

☐ Straight pins

☐ Sewing thread and needle or sewing machine

1. Cut a strip of woven fabric the width and length of the decorative portion of your current strap to act as a base for the patchwork (fig. 1). Cut the same size strip from your knit fabric.

2. Cut various pieces of patchwork fabrics. Lay them out along the base fabric strip to cover it. The edges of patches should overlap about ¼" (6 mm). The edges that align with the long edge of the base strip can be cut with straight scissors. Cut the other sides of the patches with pinking shears if possible to keep fraying in check (fig. 2).

3. Use two strips of fusible bonding tape and a warm iron to attach the patchwork squares to the base fabric one by one (fig. 3).

Fig. 1: Cut strips of knit fabric and woven cotton fabric.

Fig. 2: Cut the patchwork squares.

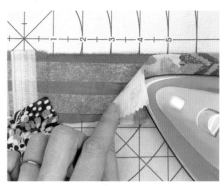

Fig. 3: Fuse the patches to the base fabric.

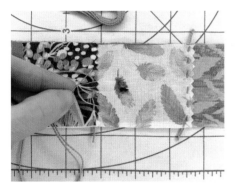

Fig. 4: Stitch the edges.

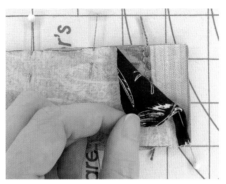

Fig. 5: Pin the front and back strips together.

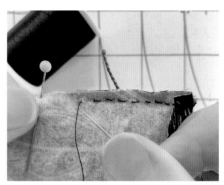

Fig. 6: Stitch the front and back together. Turn the cover right-side out.

4. Use various colors of embroidery floss to make a running stitch at each patch edge across the strap (fig. 4). Be careful to stitch through both layers of overlapping patches at each location. Leave loose ends free at either side.

5. Pin the knit fabric strip to the patch-work strip, right sides together (fig. 5). Fold and press under the short ends about ¼" (6 mm) each so the raw edges will roll under on the finished strap cover.

6. Use a small running stitch or back stitch to sew the front and back side of the strap cover together (fig. 6). Stitch close to the edge, being sure to catch all the fabric layers. You can use a sewing machine for this step if you have one. Turn the strap cover right-side out. Fold the tube outward on itself—as though you were turning a sock right side out—and keep working with your fingers until the whole strap is turned. Slide the strap cover onto your strap! The stretch of the knit fabric makes it work!

NOW TRY THIS!

This same idea can be used to freshen up camera straps for photographers or even gym bag straps for athletes.

MARBLED PAPER
NOTECARDS

Make beautiful marbled paper with simple supplies. The mess is easy to clean up since it starts with shaving cream! There is no end to the color combinations and swirl patterns you can make with this technique. And folks will love receiving a handwritten note in a handmade card. Tied with a bow, sets of these cards make thoughtful gifts for teachers, family, and friends.

MATERIALS

☐ Shaving cream/foam

☐ Flat baking pan

☐ Liquid food coloring

☐ Chopstick or similar stirring tool

☐ White cardstock

☐ Cardboard strip or another scraping tool

☐ Blank notecards

☐ Glue stick

1. Spread shaving foam on the bottom of a baking pan to cover most of the bottom (fig. 1).

2. Drip a few colors of food coloring randomly on the surface of the shaving foam (fig. 2).

3. Use a chopstick to swirl the food coloring around in the foam to create an interesting pattern (fig. 3). You can add extra drops of food coloring if you find there are areas you missed. But don't stir so much that you blend everything together into one color!

Fig. 1: Make a layer of shaving foam.

Fig. 2: Add food coloring.

Fig. 3: Swirl the color.

Fig. 4: Lay down the cardstock.

Fig. 5: Remove the cardstock.

Fig. 6: Scrape the cardstock.

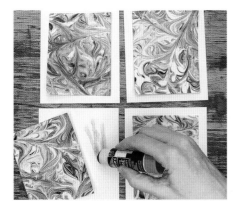

Fig. 7: Glue the marbled sheets to blank notecards.

4. Carefully lay the cardstock sheet onto the surface of the foam and press lightly to ensure good contact across the sheet (fig. 4).

5. Peel away the cardstock gently, grasping it at the corner (fig. 5). There will be lots of foam stuck to your sheet.

6. Use a strip of stiff cardboard or another straight-edge tool to scrape the foam off of the cardstock into a sink or spare pan (fig. 6). This will reveal your marbled design! Lay the sheet face up to dry.

7. Once dry, trim the marbled sheets as necessary and glue to blank notecards with a glue stick (fig. 7).

Express Yourself

You are a creative being. You look at the world and imagine things as they could be. You put your unique stamp on everything you touch. That's what it means to express yourself! So add some flair and signature colors to your jeans with splashes of paint. Make a colorful, tactile monogram for your bedroom wall. Write down your most poetic thoughts and weave them into a meaningful bracelet. The world craves and needs individuals who are unafraid to be themselves. Crafting is one amazing way to put yourself out there. Be authentic. Be brave and confident in your uniqueness. Be YOU!

Look like you've been in the studio all your life painting masterpieces. These painter's jeans are stylish, artsy, and full of personality. Add a splash of your favorite colors to your closet.

Use dry brushing, dripping, and spattering for a design guaranteed to be an original.

MATERIALS

- ☐ Drop cloth, newspaper, or plastic tablecloth
- ☐ Old jeans
- ☐ Craft paints *(various colors)*
- ☐ Cups or bowls *(disposable paper products work fine)*
- ☐ Paper plates
- ☐ Paintbrushes in various sizes
- ☐ Spoons
- ☐ Old toothbrush

1. Lay out a drop cloth, newspaper, or plastic tablecloth to protect your work area (fig. 1). Lay down the jeans and smooth out any wrinkles.

2. Start with some messy white paint to establish the main area to be painted (fig. 2). This is typically about hip to knee, since that's where a painter would actually wipe their hands while painting. Work quickly to add messy, haphazard strokes of white paint straight from the bottle.

3. Squirt a few colors of craft paint onto the paper plate. Layer about three to four colors onto the jeans, one at a time (fig. 3). Go all different directions and work quickly without overthinking. Change brushes and make the strokes deliberate—don't try to blend. Holding a long-handled brush at the end of the handle can help free up your movements and strokes. Adding just a few stray strokes on the seams, near the pockets and waistband, and closer to the ankles will make the design look more free and loose.

Fig. 1: Protect the work area.

Fig. 2: Paint on some white brushstrokes.

Fig. 3: Add colors.

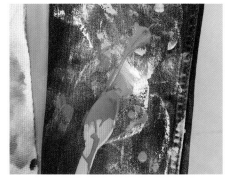

Fig. 4: Drizzle, scrape, and spatter paint that has been slightly thinned with water.

Fig. 5: Add more white.

Fig. 6: Flick on some gold paint.

4. For the dripping and spattering, you will need to add a small amount of water to your paints. You can do this in a small cup. Paints should be pourable but not watery. Stir in a few drops of water at a time to get the right consistency. Use a spoon to scoop a little paint and drizzle it across the jeans. You can drag the spoon through any large splatters and scrape it in a line for interest. Scoop up a little paint with the spoon and flick it onto the jeans to make droplets. The higher you hold the spoon, the smaller the drops will be. Holding the spoon closer to the jeans results in larger drops (fig. 4).

5. Add some white back onto a few damp areas of color with a light scribble or swipe motion (fig. 5). This will make a blended, brighter pastel version of the color and really make the pattern look realistic and alive.

6. Use an old toothbrush to flick on some metallic gold paint to finish it all off (fig. 6). Hold the brush very close to the jeans and run your thumb along the bristles with a hard, fast motion.

NOW TRY THIS!

You can try this on white painter's pants, a denim jacket, or a bag too. A canvas tote painted this way would be perfect for hauling your sketchbook and other art supplies around town.

DIP-DYED CANVAS BACKPACK

Fabric dye works wonders. It really can turn something dull and boring into something colorful and interesting. Dip-dyeing is especially fun because it's always a bit of an experiment. It's great for a beginner because you can achieve lots of nice layers with just one bucket of dye by simply varying the amount of time parts of the fabric are allowed to soak. This quick two-step dipped backpack project is the perfect primer.

MATERIALS

☐ Cotton canvas bag

☐ Straight pins

☐ Hanger (optional)

☐ Rubber gloves

☐ Fabric dye (one color)

☐ Large bucket or pot

☐ Drop cloth

1. Wash the bag to remove any chemicals or finishes and leave it damp. Place pins on both sides of the bag, two pins about one-quarter of the way up the bag and two more halfway up the bag (fig. 1). It may be helpful to clip the bag to a hanger for dipping. It will give you something to hold onto and will keep the bag level.

2. Put on rubber gloves! Dye will stain your skin. Mix the dye in the large bucket according to package directions (fig. 2). Work outside or with a drop cloth to avoid staining from splashes.

3. Dip the damp bag into the dye up to the top set of pins (fig. 3). The dampness of the bag will help the dye spread upward, creating a soft fade rather than a crisp edge of color. Leave the bag dipped at this level for 2 minutes.

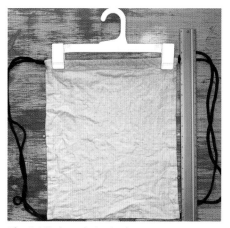

Fig. 1: Wash and pin the bag.

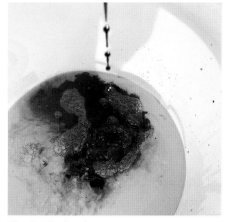

Fig. 2: Mix the dye.

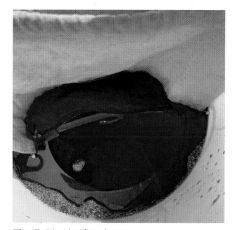

Fig. 3: Dip the first layer.

Fig. 4: Dip the second layer.

Fig. 5: Rinse the bag.

Fig. 6: Let the bag dry.

4. Raise the bag up so that the water level is at the bottom set of pins (fig. 4). Leave the bag dipped at this level for 8 minutes. (You can adjust the times a little depending on how well your color dye is absorbing into the fabric.)

5. Rinse the bag until the water runs clear (fig. 5). Make sure to run the water downward so dye is not transferred to the top part of the bag.

6. Dry the bag in the sun or dryer according to package instructions (fig. 6). Set the color if directed.

NOW TRY THIS!

Try dip-dyeing a T-shirt or skirt in your team color.

YARN-WRAPPED WIRE INITIAL

Monograms and initials are always a great way to personalize a space. This project turns your handwriting into a colorful, decorative initial to brighten up a bookshelf or wall. Using your own handwriting, not a computer font, is what makes it most special. You capture a bit of yourself in the process. The results are so much more unique this way and really make a memory.

MATERIALS

☐ Marker

☐ Paper

☐ Ruler or tape measure

☐ Armature wire *(the thicker the better)*

☐ Wire cutters

☐ Masking tape

☐ Variegated yarn

☐ White glue

1. Write your initial in your own hand-writing on a sheet of paper (fig. 1). Make it about 10" (25 cm) high.

2. Bend some wire to the approximate length you'll need for your letter and cut it with wire cutters (fig. 2). If you need additional lengths for smaller parts of the letter, cut those too.

3. Use your hands to bend the wire into shape, using the drawing as your guide (fig. 3). Armature wire is very pliable and easy to manipulate.

4. Use masking tape to attach any small wire parts of your letter (fig. 4). Also wrap the cut ends to dull any sharp edges and make them bulky enough to accept the glue and end wraps of yarn.

Fig. 1: Draw your initial.

Fig. 2: Cut the wire.

Fig. 3: Shape the parts of the letter.

Fig. 4: Tape the letter.

Fig. 5: Glue the yarn. Wrap the letter.

Fig. 6: Finish with a knot.

5. Cut about 1 yard (1 m) of yarn and glue the end to the masking tape on one end of your letter. Hold it in place a few seconds before beginning to wrap yarn over the glued end to conceal it. Continue wrapping the wire with yarn. Remember to push back the coils of yarn along the wire as you go to make them very densely packed. When you run out of yarn, cut a new length, apply glue, and proceed as you did with the first piece: glue, hold, then wrap over the end to conceal. Continue until the whole letter is wrapped (fig. 5).

6. End the wrapping by pulling the tail through one of the loops you've made while wrapping. Pull tight (fig. 6). Add a drop of glue and wrap two more times, then trim the tail and hold it down with another drop of glue. Hold until it sets and stays in place.

NOW TRY THIS!

- Prop your initial on a bookshelf or hang it on the wall with a bit of ribbon or string.

- Challenge yourself to create your entire signature with wire and wrap that! Use metallic thread or yarn for a bit of sparkle.

PHOTO-TRANSFER
MEMORY BOX

Photo transfer is a little like magic. It is a very rewarding craft and incredibly fun to see the image revealed on the wood. Make a memory box for your best friend with a photo of the two of you on the front. Fill it with mementos of experiences you've shared, like movie stubs, friendship bracelets from camp, science fair ribbons, and more. Or create a box with you and your siblings to give as a Mother's or Father's Day gift.

MATERIALS

☐ Small unfinished wood box

☐ Paintbrush

☐ Decoupage medium

☐ Photo *(printed with a laser printer at the right size for your box)*

☐ Heavy books

☐ Wood stain or paint

☐ Sealer *(optional)*

1. Use a paintbrush to apply an even layer of decoupage medium to the top of the wooden box (fig. 1).

2. Place the laser-printed photo face down on the decoupage medium (fig. 2). Gently smooth the paper to get good contact in all areas. If there are parts of the paper that don't make good contact with the wood, you will see gaps in your finished transfer. Press down firmly and try not to shift the paper side to side to prevent blurring of the transferred image.

3. Allow the box to dry for 24 hours, weighted down with heavy books (fig. 3).

4. After the box is dry, wet the surface of the paper evenly with your fingers (fig. 4). Keep adding water until it soaks through and you can start to see the image.

5. Use your fingers to begin rubbing off the wet paper (fig. 5). Be gentle. It may take a few rounds of rubbing and allowing to dry. When dry, it's more obvious where some paper is still adhered. Wet that area once more and try again.

Fig. 1: Brush on the decoupage medium.

Fig. 2: Apply the photo.

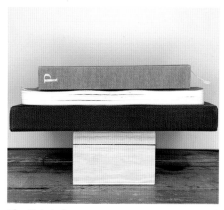

Fig. 3: Let dry.

Fig. 4: Apply water.

Fig. 5: Rub off the paper.

Fig. 6: Stain the box.

Fig. 7: Seal the box.

6. Apply wood stain (or paint if you prefer) to the sides and interior of the box (fig. 6).

7. Apply varnish or other sealer to the box sides and interior (fig. 7), if you like.

NOW TRY THIS!

Try distressing your transferred images for an aged and weathered look. Simply rub certain areas of the image off intentionally in the paper removal step or even use sandpaper when it's dry to create blank patches and worn edges on the photo.

MINI WALL WEAVING

Once you learn weaving, you won't be able to stop! This craft employs a beginner's weaving technique to make a simple wall hanging, but there are countless variations you can learn once you master the basics. Weaving takes time and patience. So grab a friend and a snack to work on this one afternoon. Your finished wall hanging will be well worth it!

MATERIALS

☐ Cardboard

☐ Pencil

☐ Ruler or tape measure

☐ Scissors

☐ Yarn in a few colors

☐ Plastic needle with a large eye

☐ Masking tape

☐ Chopstick or small dowel

NOW TRY THIS!

Using a variety of yarn textures and thicknesses will give your weavings wonderful dimension. Add in some metallic threads for a bit of sparkle as well!

Fig. 1: Make the loom.

Fig. 2: Wrap the warp yarns vertically.

Fig. 3: Begin weaving.

1. Cut a piece of cardboard about 5″ × 6″ (13 × 15 cm). Make pencil marks ¼″ (6 mm) apart across both the top and bottom and snip notches into them with scissors (fig. 1).

2. Starting at the bottom left, leave about an 8″ (20 cm) tail and tuck the yarn into the first notch on the lower left and up into the first notch at the upper left. Loop it around the back and through the second bottom notch (fig. 2). Continue across the loom and then tie off the tails in the back.

3. Use a plastic needle threaded with about 1 yard (1 m) of your first color of yarn to begin an over-and-under pattern across the warp (vertical) yarns (fig. 3). Leave a few inches (7 cm) of tail as you begin. When you get to the end of a row, loop the yarn back over or under the last warp strand and create the next row going back the other direction. Continue for as many rows as you like, then change to a new color using the same steps.

(continued)

Fig. 4: Tighten your weave as you add colors.

Fig. 5: Release the weaving.

Fig. 6: Tie off the warp yarns in pairs.

4. Continually use your fingers to push the weft (horizontal) yarns tightly against each other along the warp (vertical) yarns to keep the weaving dense and to conceal the warp yarns (fig. 4). Do this each time you start a new color yarn. Continue to leave the tails of each new yarn strand loose at the sides of your weaving.

5. Snip through the middle of the warp threads on the back of the loom (fig. 5). Spread your weaving out so that tails are extending from each side.

6. Tie off the top and bottom warp yarns in pair of two (fig. 6). If you have an odd number, you can double up on the last knot.

Fig. 7: Weave in the weft yarns on the back side.

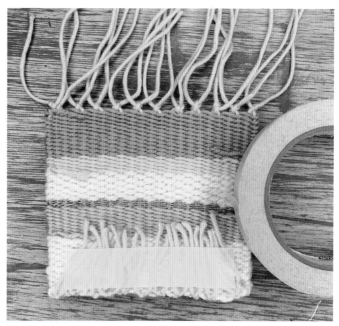

Fig. 8: Conceal the warp yarn tails on the back.

Fig. 9: Attach the rod.

7. Thread each of the weft (horizontal) yarn tails through the plastic needle one at a time. Gently weave them through a few of the yarns on the back of your weaving to conceal them (fig. 7).

8. Conceal the wrap yarn tails on the back of your weaving using the threading technique show in step 7, or simply use masking tape if you like (fig. 8). Accomplished weavers will want the clean finish, but younger kids can use the tape method for their beginning attempts.

9. Thread the plastic needle with more yarn and sew through the top of the weaving in a looping stitch to attach a dowel or chopstick at the top edge (fig. 9). Add a piece of yarn for hanging and some homemade tassels from Lab 6 to complete your wall art!

HIDDEN-MEANING FABRIC SCRAP
BRACELET

This artsy bracelet is not only stylish, but it is also full of meaning and sentiment. Use a few scraps of fabric and a whole lot of heart to create this craft with your own written words braided right in. You can choose to keep the hidden words a secret or share them on an accompanying notecard to give as a gift. Either way, it should bring a smile and fond memory every time it is worn.

MATERIALS

☐ Fabric strips (one solid and another with an interesting print)

☐ Tape measure

☐ Scissors

☐ Masking tape

☐ Fabric pens or permanent marker

☐ Needle and thread

☐ Bracelet end caps and closure

☐ Adhesive or wire

☐ Jewelry pliers

1. Cut three strips of fabric, leaving raw edges (fig. 1). Strips should measure 1" (2.5 cm) wide by about 12 to 14" (30 to 36 cm) long. One strip should be a solid color, but the two others can be prints.

2. Tear off a length of masking tape and apply it to the solid fabric strip (fig. 2). This will make it very stable while you write on the opposite side.

3. With the masking-tape-side down, write a special message, wish, prayer, poem, or inspirational quote on the solid fabric strip with a fabric pen (fig. 3).

4. Remove the masking tape from the solid fabric strip (fig. 4).

5. Use a needle and thread to stitch and wrap the fabric strip ends together (fig. 5). Knot the thread and snip.

6. Use masking tape to hold the stitched end of the strips down to the table. Braid the fabrics together, scrunching and twisting as you go to show off the prettiest colors and patterns (fig. 6). Tie off the end when you reach an appropriate length for your wrist (just as you did the first end) and snip.

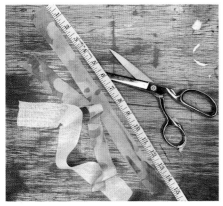
Fig. 1: Cut the fabric strips.

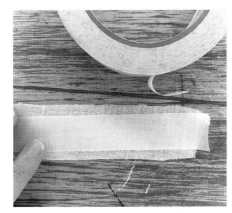
Fig. 2: Stabilize the solid fabric strip.

Fig. 3: Write on the strip.

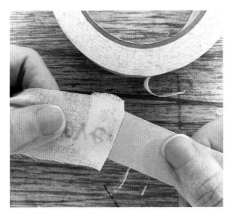
Fig. 4: Remove the tape.

Fig. 5: Stitch the strips together.

Fig. 6: Braid the strips.

Fig. 7: Add jewelry hardware.

7. Feed the ends of the braided bracelet into jewelry end caps and secure with adhesive or wire (fig. 7). Attach a clasp. Tie on a little fabric fringe for an extra pretty touch.

NOW TRY THIS!

Make this a gift from a group of friends by writing on *all* the strips. You can even double up on strips if it's from a large group. Use two strips for each section of the braid. It is sure to be a cherished memento. Include a printed card with all the messages written out, if you wish.

SHRINK PLASTIC
CHARM BRACELET

If you are looking for a fun project for all ages, this is it! Shrink film is easy to work with and so fascinating to watch! Kids love stringing beads and making something they can wear proudly right away. This simple project packs a real wow factor without much difficulty, and the opportunity to express individuality is endless.

MATERIALS

☐ Shrink film sheets

☐ Pencil

☐ Small roll of tape or lid *(for tracing)*

☐ Sandpaper

☐ Good-quality colored pencils or markers *(depending on the type of shrink film you have)*

☐ Scissors

☐ Hole punch

☐ Baking sheet

☐ Parchment paper

☐ Oven *(with adult supervision)*

☐ Jewelry pliers

☐ Jump rings

☐ Stretch elastic cord

☐ Wooden beads *(or any type with large holes)*

1. Draw 1.5" (4 cm) circles onto shrink film. You can trace a small roll of tape or a lid about that size to make it easy. This will help keep your charm designs the right size. Shrink film will reduce to about half its original size, so keep that in mind when creating your designs. Make enough circles for the number of charms you'd like on your finished bracelet. Use sandpaper to lightly scuff the surface of the shrink film so it will accept the colored pencil or marker better. Check the package of the particular shrink film you are using to see if this step is necessary. Some types come with a rough side already prepared for you (fig. 1).

2. Use colored pencils to create art on each of the circles you've traced (fig. 2). The designs don't have to be a circle shape, but they should fill out the overall size of each circle.

3. Use scissors to clip out each of the designs (fig. 3). You can trim the circle shape or cut around the outline of your designs. Punch a hole in each design for your jump ring. The hole will seem too large, but remember, the hole will shrink too!

Fig. 1: Mark 1.5″ (4 cm) circles on shrink film. Scuff the shrink film.

Fig. 2: Draw your designs.

Fig. 3: Trim the designs and punch holes.

Fig. 4: Line a baking sheet with parchment and bake. Watch them shrink!

Fig. 5: Add jump rings.

Fig. 6: String your bracelet.

4. Place your trimmed shrink film designs onto a baking sheet lined with parchment paper. Do not place them directly on the metal. Bake according to package directions. Be sure to turn on the oven light and watch your charms curl and shrink! This is half the fun. They may seem to curl too much at one point, but don't worry—they nearly always flatten at the last minute (fig. 4).

5. Use jewelry pliers to attach jump rings to your cooled charms (fig. 5). Choose a size compatible with the size of your beads. If you use larger beads, use larger jump rings so the charms can dangle out past the beads.

6. String beads and charms in an alternating sequence onto the elastic jewelry cord (fig. 6). Tie a sturdy triple knot when you reach the right length for your wrist and snip the tails.

NOW TRY THIS!

- Make a plain beaded bracelet and add shrink charms one at a time to commemorate special accomplishments or special events.

- Add a large keyring to the bracelet and for a fun wearable keychain wristlet!

POLYMER CLAY
ANIMAL CHARMS

You can't have a craft book without a clay project! Clay is the perfect medium for creative kids. It's fun to squish and shape. It can become anything you imagine! This beginner's project focuses on the basics of making simple animal faces with polymer clay. Then enjoy your creations as wearable art charms after a quick bake in the oven. It's the perfect starter project to get your feet wet in the world of creating with clay.

MATERIALS

- ☐ Wax-paper-wrapped cardboard work surface
- ☐ Polymer clay
- ☐ Ruler or tape measure
- ☐ Toothpicks
- ☐ Eye pins
- ☐ Baking sheet
- ☐ Parchment paper
- ☐ Oven *(with adult supervision)*
- ☐ Jewelry pliers
- ☐ Strong glue
- ☐ Jump rings
- ☐ Ribbon, cord, or necklace chain

1. Warm a piece of clay in your hands and roll an oval about ¾" (2 cm) wide for the animal head. Then roll tiny balls for the ears, eyes, snout, and nose (fig. 1). These balls will flatten and expand when you press them into place, so make them smaller than you actually want the finished shape to be. This takes practice. Don't worry if your sizes are a bit off the first time.

2. Press the ears onto each side of the head. Gentle tapping and pressing will help the clay form smooth curves. Pressing too hard will smoosh the clay and make it bumpy. Be patient. Apply the eyes fairly wide set and press gently to flatten them onto the surface of the face. Press the snout in the center of the face and flatten lightly. Add the tiny nose ball and press gently to attach, but don't flatten it too much (fig. 2).

3. Make tiny white balls about the size of a poppy seed and press them onto the black to put some sparkle in the bear's eyes. Make a tiny bow by flattening clay with your fingers, then twisting to pinch the center. Use a toothpick to press in creases, and attach it in front of one ear (fig. 3).

LITTLE HANDS

This project requires fine motor skills. Younger kids may find it easier to roll their clay flat and cut simple shapes like hearts, stars, and geometric shapes. They can still add faces to these shapes! A drinking straw or toothpick can be used to poke a hole into the clay before baking so that a ribbon can be threaded through to make a necklace.

Fig. 1: Create the basic forms.

Fig. 2: Apply the ears, eyes, snout, and nose.

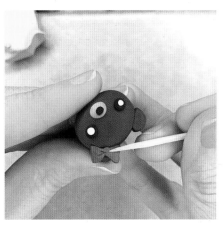
Fig. 3: Add eye highlights. Add a bow.

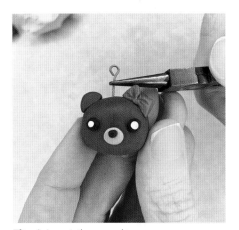
Fig. 4: Insert the eye pin.

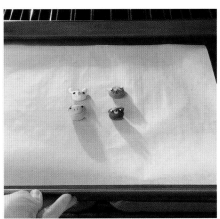
Fig. 5: Bake the clay.

Fig. 6: Glue the eye pin and add a jump ring.

4. Poke a jewelry eye pin down into the head (fig. 4). The pin will have to come out after baking and be reinserted with glue. Placing it now establishes a space for it while the clay is still soft.

5. Bake the clay according to package instructions (fig. 5). Place the figures on parchment paper on a baking sheet. (Aluminum foil will leave shiny areas on the clay.) When the time is up, turn off the oven and allow the charms to slowly come to room temperature in the oven. This helps make them especially sturdy. And when in doubt on baking times, lower temperatures for longer times is always preferable.

6. Once the clay is cool, remove the eye pin, dip it in strong glue, and reinsert it. Add a jump ring, and your charm is ready to add to a necklace (fig. 6)!

NOW TRY THIS!

These basic steps will work for most animals with small adaptations. Use different colors of clay and different ear shapes to make most animals. As you get more comfortable, expand beyond these basics and challenge your creativity!

Take Care of YOU

Being a kid can be a lot of fun, but your schedule can rival those of many adults at times. There are friends, sports, activities, music lessons, school, and volunteering. And while all of these are wonderful and valuable parts of growing up, sometimes you just need some me time. Why not treat yourself to a spa day at home complete with sugar scrub and a relaxing soak with a homemade bath bomb? Or clear your mind, stretch, and meditate on a beautifully painted yoga mat. You can squeeze your stress away with a handmade stress ball, or paint and sketch all day in a customized art journal. Taking the time to rest and recharge is important at any age. Invest some time in cultivating a habit of self-care and you'll be so happy you did. You'll be better able to serve your own purpose and help others as well.

FIZZY BATH BOMBS

Bath bombs turn your tub into a full spa experience, complete with aromatherapy! They are highly entertaining to watch as they fizz and bubble away in the water. You can make a big stash of bath bombs at home for a fraction of what they cost in the store. And you can customize the color and scent any way you like. This project has self-care written all over it. Bath bombs are fun to make, relaxing to use, and leave your craft space smelling wonderful. That's a win-win-win!

MATERIALS

- ☐ 2 cups (440 g) baking soda
- ☐ 1 cup (128 g) cornstarch
- ☐ 1 cup (240 g) Epsom salt
- ☐ 4 teaspoons coconut oil
- ☐ 10 to 20 drops essential oil
- ☐ 2 teaspoons water
- ☐ Food coloring *(optional)*
- ☐ Protective gloves
- ☐ 1 cup (250 g) citric acid
- ☐ Bath bomb molds or a muffin tin

LITTLE HANDS

Let little ones choose small plastic toys to hide in the center of each bomb. They will have fun guessing which prize will emerge in the bath.

1. Combine the baking soda, cornstarch, and Epsom salt in a large bowl (fig. 1).

2. Combine the coconut oil, essential oil, water, and food coloring, if using, in a small dish and stir (fig. 2).

3. Using gloved hands, add the wet ingredients to the dry and combine with your fingers (fig. 3).

4. Add the citric acid to the mixture and work it patiently until it comes together like wet sand (fig. 4).

Fig. 1: Mix the dry ingredients except citric acid.

Fig. 2: Mix the wet ingredients.

Fig. 3: Combine the wet and dry ingredients.

Fig. 4: Add the citric acid.

Fig. 5: Pack the molds.

Fig. 6: Assemble the molds.

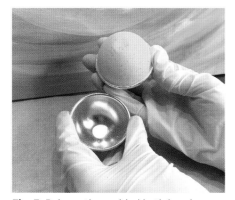

Fig. 7: Release the molded bath bombs.

5. Mound the mixture into the two halves of the bath bomb mold (fig. 5).

6. Squeeze the two sides of the mold together to form a ball (fig. 6). Press out the excess and brush it away with your fingers. Set aside for a minute or two.

7. Carefully remove the top part of the mold (fig. 7). Flip the bottom gently into your hand and set the bath bomb on parchment paper to dry for about 48 hours. Wrap in tissue for gift giving, or take a bomb for a spin in the tub!

NOW TRY THIS!

- Muffin tins make a good substitute if you don't have bath bomb molds. Place a cookie sheet on top and flip both sheet and muffin tin together when you turn the bombs out from the tin.

- Mini muffin tins make the perfect size bombs for a soothing foot soak.

HOMEMADE
SUGAR SCRUB

It's never too early to start a good skincare routine. This exfoliating sugar scrub has a great texture perfect for sloughing off those dead skin cells from heels, hands and face. The coconut-oil base leaves your skin feeling super soft. Whip up a batch with friends using ingredients you likely have in your kitchen cabinet and have a spontaneous spa party! Or wrap up a pretty jar with ribbon to give as a sweet-as-sugar gift.

MATERIALS

☐ ⅓ cup (73 g) coconut oil *(cold-pressed organic is recommended)*

☐ Mixing bowl

☐ ¾ cup (150 g) white sugar

☐ ¼ cup (50 g) coarse raw sugar

☐ Spoon

☐ 8 to 10 drops essential oil *(optional)*

1. If your coconut oil is solid at room temperature, add it to a microwave-safe container and microwave for a few seconds to get it to a pourable consistency but not steaming hot. Pour it into a mixing bowl (fig. 1).

2. Add the white sugar to the bowl with the oil (fig. 2).

3. Add the raw sugar to the bowl. This sugar adds a bit more scrubbing power because of the larger granules. It's great for hands and heels. If you want to use your scrub on your face only or have sensitive skin, you can skip the coarse sugar and use an extra ¼ cup (50 g) white sugar (fig.3).

4. Add 8 to 10 drops of essential oil to the bowl and mix thoroughly (fig. 4).

Note: Read the label on your essential oil and always be sure to use oils that are safe for direct application to the skin.

5. Scoop your scrub into jars or any airtight container to store (fig. 5).

Fig. 1: Melt the coconut oil.

Fig. 2: Add the white sugar.

Fig. 3: Add the coarse raw sugar.

Fig. 4: Add essential oil for aromatherapy (optional).

Fig. 5: Portion into airtight jars.

NOW TRY THIS!

- Add food coloring for a pretty tint to your scrub. Stick to just a drop or two. Less dye is better for your skin!

- Make a rainbow of sugar scrubs and gift each of your friends their favorite color and scent.

- Experiment with other oils like jojoba, olive, avocado, and grapeseed to see which you like best!

HAND-PAINTED MANDALA
YOGA MAT

Yoga and meditation are good for your body and your mind. You may as well have a beautiful yoga mat beneath you while you practice. This painted yoga mat looks intricate but is actually composed of very simple shapes that anyone can create. It's the repetition of the shapes that creates such a beautiful result. The bonus of this project is that the actual process of painting a mandala like this is meditative and relaxing. It's got self-care built right in!

MATERIALS

☐ Pencil

☐ String

☐ Yoga mat

☐ Washable marker

☐ Acrylic paint *(craft or artist-grade paints work fine)*

☐ Paintbrush

☐ Paper towel

Teachable Moment

This project is a marriage of art and math. Bisecting angles at each step of the design process make the mandala's symmetry possible. Drawing the circle guides with the homemade compass requires an understanding of circle radius. Love of mathematics and love of art are not as opposite as they may seem!

Fig. 1: Tie a string around a pencil.

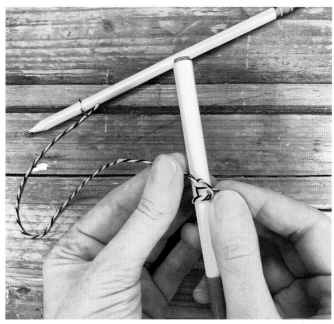
Fig. 2: Tie the other end of the string to a marker.

Fig. 3: Draw a circle.

1. Knot some string around a sharpened pencil, which will serve as the anchor for your compass (fig. 1).

2. Snip your string to about half the width of the yoga mat. Then tie the loose end to a washable marker (fig. 2). Choose a color similar to the yoga mat color so it isn't too noticeable. Note: The amount of string that is used to tie on the marker will shorten the string a little. That's perfect. You want the largest circle you draw to be an inch or two (a few centimeters) narrower than the mat.

3. Place the tip of the pencil exactly in the center of the yoga mat. You may need a helper to keep it steady as you extend the string and draw a circle with your homemade compass (fig. 3).

(continued)

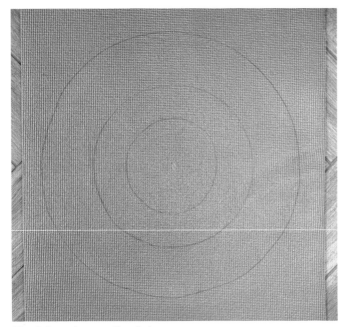

Fig. 4: Draw two smaller circles.

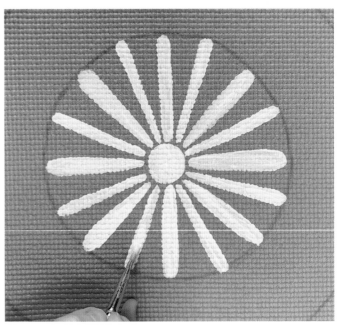

Fig. 5: Paint the center flower.

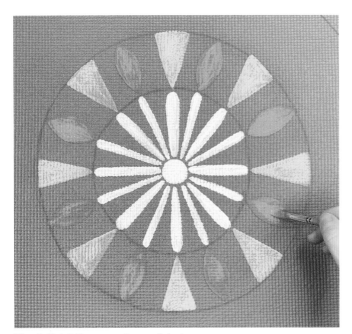

Fig. 6: Paint the second row of designs.

4. Shorten the string about 3″ (7.5 cm) and draw a circle, then shorten it again by 3″ (7.5 cm) and draw another circle (fig. 4). You don't need to be exact. The circle guides will just help your mandala stay symmetrical.

5. Paint a dot in the center. Then add slim petals like a daisy, filling the smallest circle (fig. 5). It's easy to keep spacing consistent if you paint the first four petals like a cross, two vertical and two horizontal. Paint the next set of petals in the center of the remaining spaces, and so on.

6. Paint triangles using the middle circle guide. Think of a clock face and paint them at 12, 3, 6, and 9. Then add four more, centered in the spaces left behind. Finally, add petal/football shapes in a different color between the triangles (fig. 6).

Fig. 7: Paint the third row of designs.

Fig. 8: Add finishing touches.

Fig. 9: Wipe off the marker guides.

7. Paint arches like a rainbow from triangle to triangle. Add three brushstrokes between the arches as shown (fig. 7). Then pick another color and paint another set of arches over those little brushstrokes. Finish with more little brushstrokes between the second set of arches.

8. Jazz up your design any way you like (fig. 8). Paint centers in the pink petals. Add dots in the second row. Use your creativity here!

9. Once the paint is fully dry, dampen a paper towel and wipe off the circle guides (fig. 9).

JIGGLY SOAP

Crafting is extra fun when the clean-up is built right in! These jiggly soaps are so easy to make, and cleanup is a breeze, because all the mess is soap! It's likely that you have all the ingredients you need in your kitchen and bathroom cabinets. Unflavored gelatin and any sort of liquid soap are the star ingredients. You can even use shampoo! Getting washed up will be a blast with these fun soaps that wiggle and wobble. Remember these are for bathing, not eating!

MATERIALS

☐ Mixing bowl

☐ 2 packets (0.25 ounces [7 g] each) unflavored gelatin

☐ ½ cup (120 ml) boiling water

☐ Spoon

☐ 1 teaspoon salt

☐ ¾ cup (180 ml) liquid hand soap or shampoo

☐ Food coloring

☐ Silicone soap or candy mold

☐ Rubbing alcohol in a spray bottle *(optional)*

1. In a medium bowl, mix two packets of unflavored gelatin powder in the boiling water. Stir to dissolve (fig. 1).

2. Stir in the salt (fig. 2).

3. Add the liquid soap and stir to combine (fig. 3).

4. Add food coloring and stir *gently* so you don't cause too many bubbles (fig. 4). You may choose to divide the mixture into smaller bowls so you can make multiple colors.

Fig. 1: Dissolve the gelatin powder.

Fig. 2: Add the salt.

Fig. 3: Add the liquid soap.

Fig. 4: Add the food coloring.

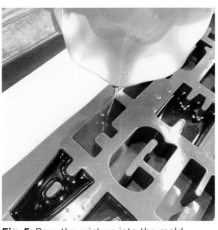

Fig. 5: Pour the mixture into the mold.

Fig. 6: Pop the soaps out of the mold and lather up.

5. Pour the soap mixture into your silicone mold (fig. 5). If you don't have a silicone mold, plastic cups can substitute. Any flexible container that will allow you to pop the soaps out is a good bet. If you use plastic cups, cut them down to about 1″ (2.5 cm) tall to make removal easier. Pop the mold into the refrigerator for 2 hours or more to set. If you like, spritz some rubbing alcohol from a spray bottle to pop bubbles on the surface of the poured soap. It lowers the surface tension of the bubbles and makes them collapse!

6. Remove the soaps from the mold by pressing on the back of each form. Keep the soaps stored in the fridge in a covered dish when not in use. Enjoy (fig. 6)!

NOW TRY THIS!

Try pouring multiple colors into each soap mold for a fun effect.

DIY STRESS BALLS

Make your own squishy stress ball with just a few simple ingredients. It's a fun and entertaining fidget toy to squeeze and squish anytime, or it can keep you distracted and calm in stressful situations.

MATERIALS

- ☐ Balloons
- ☐ 2 cups (256 g) cornstarch
- ☐ 1 cup (235 ml) water
- ☐ Bowl or large measuring cup
- ☐ Spoon
- ☐ Empty plastic water bottle
  (the thin plastic kind that collapses easily works best)

1. Combine the cornstarch and water in a bowl or a large measuring cup with a handle and spout to make pouring easier (fig. 1). Stir slowly until the mixture is homogeneous. Be patient. It seems difficult to stir at first but will quickly come together.

2. Pour the cornstarch mixture into the empty water bottle (fig. 2). Work slowly and carefully. It can get messy!

3. Stretch the balloon collar onto the water bottle, flip it upside-down, and fill the balloon with the mixture by gently squeezing the bottle (fig. 3). One recipe is enough for about two stress balls. Don't overfill!

4. Pinch the balloon neck, then turn the bottle right-side up before removing the balloon (fig. 4). You don't want any air in the balloon. Knot the balloon tightly against the contents.

5. Squish, squeeze, and scrunch your way to relaxation (fig. 5)!

Fig. 1: Mix the cornstarch and water together.

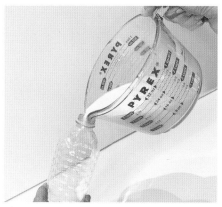

Fig. 2: Pour the mixture into a plastic bottle.

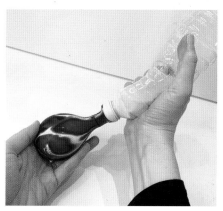

Fig. 3: Fill the balloon with the mixture.

Fig. 4: Remove the balloon from the bottle and tie a knot in the balloon.

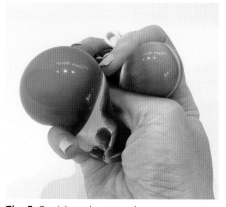

Fig. 5: Squish and squeeze!

EXTRA HELP

Lay out newspaper on your work surface. The mixture is bizarre and doesn't clean up like a liquid or solid does. I've found scraping any spills with a drywall trowel right into a trash bag is the most effective. We scraped up a popped stress ball from a tile floor, then used an old toothbrush to loosen the remaining cornstarch residue, and finally vacuumed. It was oddly entertaining! Kids should play with their stress balls outside if possible to avoid messy accidents.

When the stress balls are left to sit for a while, they will feel like they've solidified. But it's not permanent! If you gently start to work and squeeze them, they will come back to squishy consistency again. Keep your stress ball no more than 3 to 5 days before discarding.

SOFT FLEECE SLEEP MASK

This soft and cozy sleep mask is sure to give you sweet dreams. A little fabric glue and some quick stitches are all it takes. Choose fun fabrics and trims to personalize your design. Putting it together is so quick and easy, you'll want to make a few extras to share with your friends. It's the perfect craft for a sleepover or camp out with style!

MATERIALS

☐ Glasses or sunglasses

☐ Paper or cardstock

☐ Pencil

☐ Scissors

☐ Dressmaker pins

☐ Fleece fabric

☐ Fabric glue

☐ Mini pompom trim

☐ Scrap of black felt

☐ Elastic band

☐ Needle and thread

1. Trace around a pair of glasses or sunglasses to make a template on cardstock (fig. 1). Draw your outline ½" (1 cm) or more outside the perimeter of the glasses. Use scissors to cut out the cardstock template.

2. Use dressmaker pins to secure the template to two layers of fleece. Use scissors to cut through both layers (fig. 2).

3. Use fabric glue to attach the two fleece layers together for a fluffy sleep mask that blocks more light than a single layer (fig. 3). You can stitch the two layers together if you prefer. Just keep stitching very close to the edge.

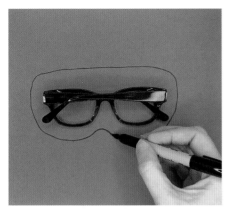

Fig. 1: Make your template.

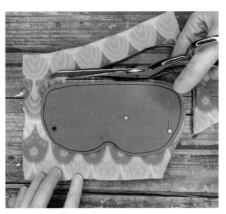

Fig. 2: Pin the template and cut the fleece.

Fig. 3: Glue the layers.

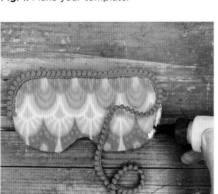

Fig. 4: Apply the pompom trim.

Fig. 5: Snip and glue the eyelashes.

Fig. 6: Attach the elastic band.

4. Glue the pompom trim along the edge of the sleep mask (fig. 4). Be sure to press firmly so the trim is secure.

5. Snip some silly eyelashes from black felt and attach it to the mask with fabric glue (fig. 5).

6. Stitch one end of your elastic to the back left side of the sleep mask. Try it for size to mark a good length of elastic for your head. Snip the elastic to length and stitch the other end to the back right side of the mask (fig. 6).

NOW TRY THIS!

- Match a sleep mask to your favorite pajamas or robe.

- Make a reversible sleep mask by choosing a different fabric for each side.

EASY-SEW POCKET WARMERS

Stay toasty warm this winter with these quick and easy-to-make pocket warmers. Two pieces of fabric, some stitching, and some uncooked rice are all it takes to make these cute and comforting pouches. Pop them in the microwave for 30 seconds or so, then tuck them into your coat pockets before you head out to for the bus stop, a football game, or a jog in the park. They're so simple and so useful, you'll want some for every coat in your closet!

MATERIALS

☐ Paper

☐ Ruler or tape measure

☐ Scissors or pinking shears

☐ Marker

☐ Dressmaker pins

☐ Felted wool, cotton flannel, or cotton fleece fabric

☐ Pinking shears or scissors

☐ Needle

☐ Cotton embroidery floss or heavy cotton thread

☐ Uncooked rice

1. Draw a shape for your warmer on paper. Be sure the warmer will fit into your coat pocket. About 4" to 5" (10 to 13 cm) is usually a good size. Simple shapes work best for ease of stitching and filling. Cut out the pattern (fig. 1).

2. Use dressmaker pins to tack the paper pattern to a double thickness of fabric. Use pinking shears or scissors to cut out the shapes. Repeat for a total of four fabric shapes for each set (fig. 2).

3. Use a needle and thread or floss to make a running stitch around the perimeter of each pouch (fig. 3). Stop stitching when you get about 1" (2.5 cm) from the starting point.

4. Make a little paper cone and secure it with tape. Cut off the tip for an easy funnel. Insert the funnel into the pouch and fill with uncooked rice (fig. 4).

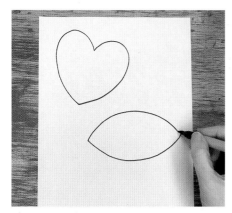

Fig. 1: Draw the pattern and cut it out.

Fig. 2: Pin the pattern to the fabric. Cut the shapes.

Fig. 3: Stitch.

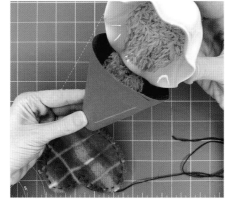

Fig. 4: Fill the pouch.

Fig. 5: Stitch and knot.

Fig. 6: Warm your pockets.

Teachable Moment

Natural fibers like cotton flannel, cotton fleece, wool, plus cotton thread, are best for this project because they won't be affected at all by microwaves. Microwave ovens heat items by exciting their molecules. For synthetic fabrics and plastics, that could mean melting or catching fire. Microwave ovens operate at 2.4GHz because that frequency works well to heat water. Most food, even food like rice that seems dry, has a high water content. The microwave's energy will be first absorbed into the rice, and the pouch itself won't even get hot. While it's unlikely that synthetic fabrics would actually melt during short spins in the microwave like this, it's better to be safe than sorry. Placing a mug of water into the microwave oven alongside the warmers each time will also act to absorb the microwave's energy, keeping the fabric pouch safe and sound.

5. Finish stitching the pouch closed and tie a knot (fig. 5). Snip the tails. Repeat all steps for the second pouch.

6. Microwave the warmers for about 30 seconds alongside a mug of water. Lessen the time if necessary, as heating times can vary with different microwaves. You want them warm, not hot. Ask an adult to help if necessary. Place the pouches in your coat pockets (fig. 6) and forget about frosty fingers this winter!

HAND-TIED
ART JOURNAL

Calling all artists! Here is the most beautiful little project to inspire your creativity through collage, sketching, painting, and more. Make your own journal full of papers you love and colors that speak to you, with a cover that is personalized and unique. You can draw and paint right on the pages, or glue in favorite drawings cut from other sketchbooks, napkins, or notebooks. Since the pages are tied together, you can add more over time or remove any you don't love.

MATERIALS

☐ Various papers for the interior

☐ Watercolor paper

☐ Lightweight cardboard (two small 6" [15 cm] squares)

☐ Tape

☐ Watercolor paint

☐ Paintbrushes

☐ Hole punch

☐ Ribbon and twine

☐ Scissors or a paper cutter

☐ Black masking tape (optional)

☐ Colored pencils (optional)

1. Choose an assortment of papers for your journal interior and cut them into 6" (15 cm) squares (fig. 1).

2. Wrap watercolor paper around two cardboard squares and tape them to make the covers (fig. 2). If you prefer to collage or use acrylic paint directly on your covers, go for it! The outside should represent YOU! This example merely shows one option.

3. Paint a design on the covers (fig. 3). Make it personal. Abstract watercolor art is shown here, but your journal should represent you and what you like to draw and paint.

4. Punch a hole in the middle/edge of one of the interior pages. Then punch two more holes on either side for a total of three holes per page (fig. 4). You can use the first punched page as a template as you work your way through punching all the others.

5. Align the covers and punch holes in those (fig. 5).

Fig. 1: Trim the interior papers.

Fig. 2: Wrap the covers.

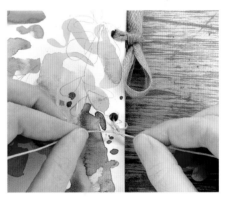
Fig. 3: Paint the covers.

Fig. 4: Punch holes in the pages.

Fig. 5: Punch holes in the covers.

Fig. 6: Tie a ribbon in the top corner. Tie the twine.

6. Thread a wide ribbon through the top corner hole of both covers and all pages. Wrap a piece of tape around the ribbon end to aid in threading it through the stack. Tie a bow or nice knot. Thread twine through the remaining holes and double knot it before snipping. Leave these twine loops a bit loose so you can turn the pages easily (fig. 6).

7. Add any touches you'd like to your cover art (fig. 7). Then, if desired, use black masking tape and a colored pencil to make a name label to finish.

Fig. 7: Add finishing touches and a name label.

LITTLE HANDS

Younger kiddos can make a chunkier simpler version of this book. Use poster board for the covers and fun, bright papers for the interior. An adult can help with the hole punching. Consider using hinged binder-type rings instead of tying ribbon and twine. The rings are easy to open and close and make turning the pages a snap.

UNIT 4

Kids Just Wanna Have Fun

The heart of any art or craft is entertainment and enjoyment. You do it for the joy it brings! So go for the fun factor and don't hold back. Blow up a ridiculous number of colorful balloons and string together a big balloon garland photo-op. There doesn't even need to be a party. Just get silly with your friends and make some cute selfie memories! Or maybe break out the confetti (literally) with candy-stuffed party poppers. They are fun for all ages! Become a tic-tac-toe champion during your next road trip or the piñata master this coming birthday! Make miles of pompom garland just because it makes you grin ear to ear. At the end of the day, your memories will be made in moments of laughter and silliness. Create opportunities for fun and play every day.

You know how to throw a party! Nothing says photo-op like a balloon arch and some fun backdrops. Be sure you have lots of memories from your next celebration by giving folks the perfect place to be silly and snap some selfies. It may look complicated, but this balloon arch and backdrops are super easy to make once you know the steps. You'll have the place looking like a carnival in no time!

MATERIALS

Balloon Arch

☐ Balloons *(various colors, about 75 for the arch size shown)*

☐ Mini clear rubber bands

☐ Monofilament *(invisible nylon thread or fishing line)*

☐ Masking tape

Stars Backdrop

☐ Glitter cardstock

☐ Scissors

☐ String

☐ Plain or pink cardstock

☐ Glue

☐ Lightweight wooden dowel

Pennant Backdrop

☐ Patterned scrapbook paper

☐ Scissors or a paper cutter

☐ String

☐ Masking tape

1. Blow up three balloons and knot them. Then twist them together to make clusters (fig. 1). Secure the clusters with clear mini rubber bands.

2. Continue blowing up balloons and making clusters (fig. 2). Put together nice color combos so the arch will have evenly distributed colors.

Fig. 1: Blow up three balloons and cluster them together.

Fig. 2: Repeat step one 20 to 25 times.

3. Use the invisible monofilament to string the clusters together. In the photo, string is used for a clearer visual (fig. 3). You want to pull the fishing line into the center of each cluster and then wrap it around the knot a few times like a figure eight to be sure the cluster is secure. Have your partner hand you the next cluster and do it again.

4. Continue adding clusters until a column of balloons starts to form (fig. 4). It gets easier after the third or fourth cluster, once the structure becomes apparent. Continue until you've used all the clusters. If you need to add more fishing line length, just tie a knot around the center of your last cluster and continue. The fishing line ends are nearly impossible to see, so nobody will ever know! Hang using more fishing line looped over curtain rods or even just taped to the wall with masking tape. The arch is so light that it is easily secured.

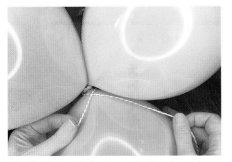

Fig. 3: String the balloon clusters together.

Fig. 4: Assemble the clusters to make a column.

BACKDROPS

Stars: Cut glitter stars and colored stars. Sandwich strands of string between them and secure with glue. Make several strands of stars and hang them from a lightweight wooden dowel. The dowel is so light that it can be taped right to the wall with painter's tape or masking tape.

Pennants: Cut triangles from patterned paper. Fold the top edges over a length of string and secure with masking tape. Add several pennants per string. Hang two strands on the wall at different angles with masking tape.

NOW TRY THIS!

- Cut hearts instead of stars for Valentine's Day.

- Spell words on your pennant banners for any occasion.

- Blow up a bunch of extra loose balloons for your balloon arch. You can scatter them on the floor for photos or let your guests play with them for some funny pics!

PARTY POPPERS

Any day is a celebration when you get to pop open an explosion of confetti and sweet treats. Make these cute and colorful party poppers for birthday parties, New Year's Eve, or any special day. They are easy for any age and use simple supplies you likely already have on hand, and assembly is mess-free aside from maybe some stray confetti.

MATERIALS

☐ Tissue paper *(the cheaper, thinner and more easily torn, the better!)*

☐ Ruler or tape measure

☐ Scissors

☐ Paper towel tubes, cut into 1½" (4 cm) lengths

☐ Glue stick

☐ Ribbon

☐ Small candies and treats

1. Cut 10 × 10" (25.5 × 25.5 cm) squares of tissue in various colors for the outer wrapper of the poppers (fig. 1).

2. Center two pieces of cardboard tube at one end of a tissue paper square (fig. 2).

3. Roll the tubes in the tissue and secure with glue stick (fig. 3).

4. Tie off one end of the tissue with ribbon to close that side of the tube (fig. 4). Knot the ribbon so it's secure.

5. Make confetti by cutting thin strips of tissue, then snipping stacks of the strips into small squares (fig. 5).

6. Fill the tube from the open end with fun treats and confetti (fig. 6).

7. Tie off the open end of the popper with a ribbon knot (fig. 7). When it's time to open the poppers, grab both ends and pull hard to make the tissue split and goodies fall out.

Fig. 1: Cut squares of tissue.

Fig. 2: Place two pieces of cardboard tube onto a tissue paper square.

Fig. 3: Roll up and glue the flap.

Fig. 4: Knot ribbon on one end.

Fig. 5: Make confetti.

Fig. 6: Add treats and confetti.

Fig. 7: Tie the popper closed.

LITTLE HANDS

If confetti making with scissors is too tough for younger kids, let them use a hole punch instead. They can punch piles of circles from shiny or colorful papers in no time. And who doesn't love using a hole punch?

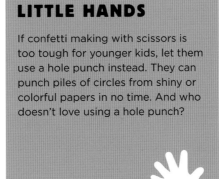

HOMEMADE RAINBOW PIÑATA

Making these box-style piñatas is so satisfying! There is no papier-mâché mess and little expense, and the possibilities for various shapes you can make are endless. It's the perfect project to tackle with a friend while watching a movie marathon. While the techniques are simple, they do take a bit of time. Settle in, enjoy the process, and get excited for amazing results. Your next party is sure to have the WOW factor when you bring out this beauty, stuffed with sweet treats.

MATERIALS

☐ Paper

☐ Pencils with new erasers

☐ 2 corrugated cardboard rectangles

☐ Scissors

☐ Masking tape

☐ Strip of corrugated cardboard
(about 4" × 45" [10 × 115 cm] long)

☐ String for hanging

☐ Crepe paper party streamers
(various colors)

☐ White glue

☐ Mylar fringe or table skirting for
hanging streamers *(optional)*

☐ Candy

Fig. 1: Create a rainbow template.

Fig. 2: Trace and cut cardboard rainbows.

1. Fold a piece of paper and draw half a rainbow on the fold. Cut and unfold so that you have a symmetrical rainbow (fig. 1).

2. Trace the rainbow shape onto the two rectangular pieces of corrugated cardboard and cut them out (fig. 2).

3. Use short strips of masking tape to attach the cardboard strip all along the edge of one rainbow cutout to form a side wall (fig. 3). Start at a lower corner so that the flap to insert candy will be in a convenient spot when you are finished.

(continued)

Fig. 3: Tape the side wall.

Fig. 4: Add a hanging loop.

Fig. 5: Cut the streamer pieces.

Fig. 6: Glue down the streamer tufts.

4. Poke two holes in the side wall at the top of the rainbow. Thread a string through and tie a knot to create a hanging loop (fig. 4).

5. Cut stacks of squares from three colors of crepe paper streamers (you'll want at least 40 to 50 squares of each color). Then cut 4″ [10 cm]–wide lengths of crepe paper and snip fringe into them for the rainbow side walls (fig. 5).

6. Rainbow stripes work better with these tufts than fringe. Wrap a square of crepe paper around a pencil eraser, dip it into white glue, and press it down onto the front of the rainbow (fig. 6). Continue gluing tufts in a stripe pattern until the whole rainbow front is filled. The secret is to press down for about 6 seconds to help it stick firmly before removing the pencil from the tuft.

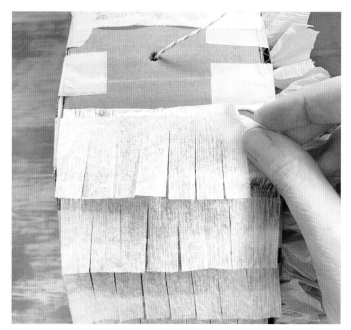

Fig. 7: Apply fringe to the side walls.

Fig. 8: Apply fringe to the back.

Fig. 9: Attach the Mylar streamer tails.

7. Starting at the bottom and working toward the top of the rainbow, glue the fringe in overlapping rows (fig. 7).

8. Cut longer strips of fringe (the width of the rainbow) and glue them on the piñata back from bottom to top in overlapping rows (fig. 8). Trim as necessary at curves.

9. Snip lengths of Mylar fringe skirting and tape it to the bottom of the piñata on each end of the rainbow (fig. 9). (You can skip this and simply cover in more fringe if you prefer.) To fill the piñata, simply snip open the masking tape where the ends of the side walls meet. Fill with candy and tape it back up. Camouflage any visible tape with extra fringe.

TRAVEL TIC-TAC-TOE

Go on a little backyard scavenger hunt to find nine similar pebbles. That's half the fun! Then turn those pebbles into cute painted Xs and Os. A drawstring pouch that you make or buy from the craft store does double duty as game board and pebble storage. This cute craft beats boredom, encourages strategic thinking, and breaks the ice when meeting new friends.

MATERIALS

☐ Masking tape or painter's tape

☐ Small drawstring pouch

☐ Craft paint (two colors, black and white shown here)

☐ Paintbrush

☐ 9 found pebbles, approximately the same size

1. Place the tape vertically onto the bag to create two vertical lines for the tic-tac-toe grid (fig. 1). Then dab the paint onto the bag in the spaces between the tape. Allow to dry and remove the tape.

2. Place the tape horizontally onto the bag to create the two horizontal lines of the tic-tac-toe grid (fig. 2). Then dab the paint onto the bag in the spaces between the tape. Allow to dry and remove the tape.

3. Paint all the pebbles black on one side and allow them to dry (fig. 3).

4. Paint all the pebbles white on the opposite side and allow them to dry (fig. 4).

Fig. 1: Tape vertical lines onto the bag and paint.

Fig. 2: Tape horizontal lines onto the bag and paint.

Fig. 3: Paint the pebbles black on one side.

Fig. 4: Paint the pebbles white on the opposite side.

Fig. 5: Paint Os on the black side.

Fig. 6: Paint Xs on the white side.

5. Use a small brush to paint white Os onto the black side of all the pebbles (fig. 5).

6. Use a small brush to paint black Xs onto the white side of all the pebbles (fig. 6).

NOW TRY THIS!

- Replace Xs and Os with initials to make a game for siblings.

- Use a slightly larger pouch and paint a grid with sixteen spaces instead of nine. Try to get four in a row instead of three.

PRETTY POMPOM GARLAND

Pompoms make everything a bit more cheerful and bright. Once you know how to make your own, you will find endless ways to use them. Sew them onto a winter hat or the corners of a throw pillow. Turn them into little pompom pets with googly eyes and felt ears. Or string them onto baker's twine as shown in this sweet pompom garland project. It's the perfect touch of color to drape on a bedroom mirror or hang at a birthday party. Go chic and monochromatic with your colors, or go full rainbow. It's up to you!

MATERIALS

☐ Yarn

☐ Ruler or tape measure

☐ Scissors

☐ Fork

☐ Baker's twine or other string

1. Cut about an 8" (20.3 cm) piece of yarn and fold it in half through the center space of the fork tines (fig. 1).

2. Use your thumb to hold the tail of your yarn against the fork and wrap about twenty-five to twenty-eight times (fig. 2). The number of wraps will depend on how fluffy and thick your yarn is and how full you want your pompom. Experiment with a few to find what works best for you.

3. Draw the 8" (20.3 cm) piece of yarn up around the center of the wrapped yarn and tie tightly (fig. 3). Double knot it as tightly as you can. This will make the best, most secure, fluffy pompom.

4. Slide the yarn off the fork and hold it close to the knot with the long tails in your palm. You don't want to snip the tails. Cut through all the loops to create the pompom tufts (fig. 4).

Fig. 1: Place the yarn in the center of the fork.

Fig. 2: Wrap the yarn around the fork.

Fig. 3: Tie the pompom.

Fig. 4: Snip the loops.

Fig. 5: Trim the pompom.

Fig. 6: Cut some twine.

Fig. 7: Assemble the garland.

5. Use scissors to trim and shape the pompom into a nice round shape (fig. 5). Repeat steps 1 through 5 many times to accumulate a big pile of pompoms!

6. Snip a piece of baker's twine about 4 feet (1.2 m) long for a nice-size garland (fig. 6). Use any length to suit your needs. The longer the twine, the more pompoms you'll need.

7. Use the yarn tails to double-knot your pompoms onto the twine. Tie them very tightly to cinch the twine in close to the center knot of the pompom (fig. 7). Snip the tails and fluff each pompom to hide the tails as you go. You will be able to slide the pompoms along the garland to get good spacing once you're all done.

WONDERFUL WANDS

Wizards, elves, fairies, and other magical characters are fun for all ages. Homemade wands are the perfect accessory. Make these imaginative props to complete a costume or just for play. The ribbon wand jingles its magic with the addition of a tiny bell. The wizard wand derives its power from the magical stone embedded in its handle. And the woodland fairy wand harnesses the power of crystals and flowers to cast its spell. There is no end to the variations and special touches you can add to these three themes. Make some magic of your own!

MATERIALS

Ribbon Wand

☐ Ribbon

☐ Ruler or tape measure

☐ D-ring

☐ Hot glue or strong glue

☐ Dowel

☐ Craft paints *(at least two colors)*

☐ Paintbrush

☐ Cotton swabs

☐ Eye hook

☐ Jingle bell

☐ Jump rings

☐ Jewelry pliers

Wizard Wand

☐ Hot glue gun or strong glue

☐ Thick stick

☐ Interesting found rock

☐ Twine

☐ Metallic gold paint

☐ Paintbrush

☐ White glue

☐ Gold glitter

Woodland Fairy Wand

☐ Silver pipe cleaners

☐ Slim, tapered twig

☐ Floral tape

☐ Artificial flowers and leaves

☐ White glue

☐ Toothpick

☐ Sparkly crystals

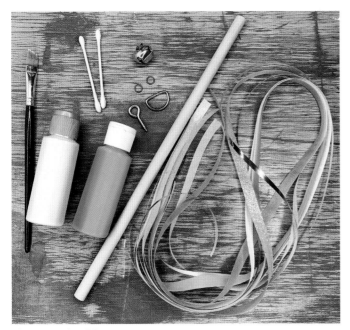

Fig. 1: Cut the ribbons.

Fig. 2: Attach the ribbons.

Fig. 3: Paint the dowel and attach the hardware, ribbon, D-ring, and bell.

RIBBON WAND

1. Cut several ribbons to about 36" (1 m) (fig. 1). Fold the bundle in half. Thread the loop through the D-ring and then pull the tails through the loop (fig. 2). Pull tight and add some hot glue or other glue to the knot to secure.

2. Paint the dowel a solid color and add dots with the cotton swab. Screw the eye hook into one end. Attach the bell and ribbon D-ring to the eye hook with jump rings (fig. 3).

(continued)

EXTRA HELP

Hot glue is really the best choice for securing the ribbon to the D-ring for the ribbon wand, and the rock to the stick for the wizard wand. Adult help handling the hot glue would be useful for this project.

Fig. 4: Glue the rock to the handle.

Fig. 5: Wrap the handle with twine.

Fig. 6: Add the metallic gold paint and glitter.

WIZARD WAND

1. Hot glue works fastest and best to attach the rock to the handle (fig. 4). You can use a different strong glue—just remember to hold it in place until it sets. Once the rock is secure, wrap the handle with twine (fig. 5). Glue down the starting end of the twine and secure it by wrapping twine over that end a few times. Crisscross the twine around the back as you surround the rock. Then glue the tail end of the twine down as well.

2. Swipe on some streaks of metallic gold paint along the wand. Cover the tip of the wand in white glue and then dip in gold glitter to finish (fig. 6).

Fig. 7: Wrap the flowers, leaves, and pipe cleaners onto the twig.

Fig. 8: Glue the crystals.

WOODLAND FAIRY WAND

1. Twist the silver pipe cleaners onto the twig in a coil shape. Then begin wrapping the twig with floral tape, starting at the bottom. Remember to stretch the floral tape as you wrap to activate the adhesive. Add in flowers and leaves as you move along the twig (fig. 7). Leave some gaps in the tape so the twig and pipe cleaner are still partially visible.

2. Use white glue applied with a toothpick to secure clusters of sparkly crystals all along the length of the wand (fig. 8).

Classic Crafts with a Twist

The classic crafts stand up to the test of time. Your great-grandmother probably created some cross-stitch back in her day, and no doubt your grandpa made some woven lanyards and God's Eyes with twigs and yarn at summer camp. Pressed flowers, embroidery, and string art have been staples for art teachers for decades. Why not honor these timeless creations by giving them a little update? Make mini versions of God's Eyes. Create T-shirt yarn for crafting those lanyards. Cross-stitch modern patterns. Turn delicate pressed flowers into stickers for your stuff. Everything old is new again, and there's a reason winning ideas always seem to come back in fashion.

GOD'S EYE MINIS

Here's a classic summer camp craft made adorably mini. God's Eyes are fun to make with inexpensive supplies. Toothpicks and thin embroidery floss keep the scale smaller than traditional God's Eyes made with dowels or twigs. These mini versions are perfect little gift toppers or even pendants. Decorate with tassels, pompoms, or anything else you can imagine. Once you start making them, you won't be able to stop!

MATERIALS

☐ White glue

☐ Toothpicks

☐ Embroidery floss *(various colors)*

☐ Masking tape

☐ Wire

☐ Scissors

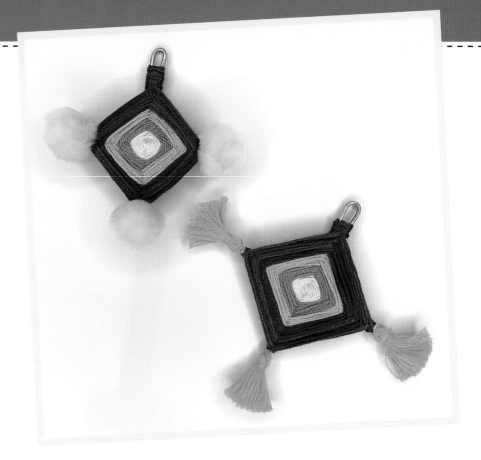

1. Dab white glue between two toothpicks to form a cross and knot one end of floss diagonally across the center (fig. 1).

2. The wrapping technique is simple once you get the hang of it. The string goes over the top of the stick, loops under, then goes back over itself toward the next stick (fig. 2).

3. Repeat the same technique of over, loop under, and cross over itself toward the next stick. Keep rotating the cross and wrapping around and around until the pattern emerges (fig. 3).

4. Change colors by tying the new color string to the original (fig. 4).

5. Continue wrapping the second color of floss the same as the first (fig. 5). Be sure to bury the knot tails toward the back as you continue to wrap in the rows of string.

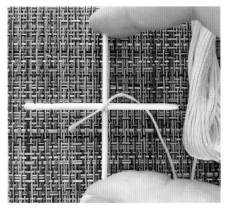

Fig. 1: Glue and tie toothpicks into a cross.

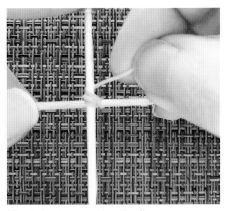

Fig. 2: Begin wrapping the floss.

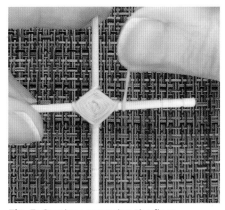

Fig. 3: Continue wrapping the floss.

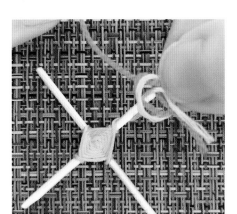

Fig. 4: Add a second color of floss.

Fig. 5: Wrap the second band of color.

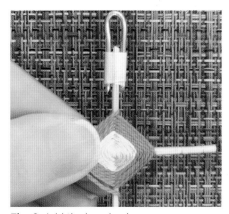

Fig. 6: Add the hanging loop.

Fig. 7: Finish wrapping the floss.

6. Bend a small piece of wire into a U shape. Glue and tape the loop onto one toothpick end, allowing good overlap of the wire and toothpick (fig. 6).

7. Continue wrapping the God's Eye until just a bit of each toothpick shows. Then wrap the "neck," where the loop is, several more times to cover (fig. 7). Tie it off and secure with white glue. Hold the tail in place for a few seconds to be sure it lays smooth. You can also add dabs of glue to the floss at the end of each toothpick to make sure they stay in place.

NOW TRY THIS!

Add mini tassels or pompoms to the exposed toothpick ends for extra style. Sparkly or wooden beads would also work well.

T-SHIRT "YARN"
BRAIDED LANYARD

Lanyards are endlessly useful. Go hands free to carry your student ID, keys, swipe cards, wallet, and more. Make this braided lanyard from an old T-shirt turned into "yarn" with a few simple snips and stretches. Printed or tie-dyed tees make multicolored yarn for a fun effect, or you can use solids to coordinate with your wardrobe. Nothing in your closet will be safe once you start making T-shirt yarn crafts like this one!

MATERIALS

☐ T-shirt

☐ Scissors

☐ Cardboard

☐ Masking tape

☐ Lanyard hardware/clip

☐ Needle and thread

☐ Fabric glue

Fig. 1: Cut the shirt.

Fig. 2: Fold the tube.

Fig. 3: Snip the strips.

Fig. 4: Open the tube.

1. Cut the hem off the tee and make another cut just under the spot where sleeves attach (fig. 1). This will leave you with a tube of knit fabric.

2. Fold the tube left to right (fig. 2).

3. Cut strips about ½" (1 cm) wide from left to right, stopping short of the folds on the right side (fig. 3).

4. Unfold the tube again so that the uncut folds are at left and right again (fig. 4).

(continued)

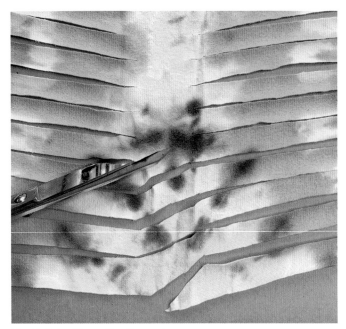

Fig. 5: Snip slits on the diagonal.

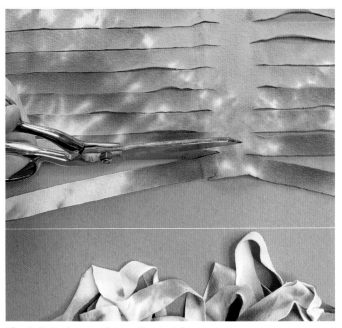

Fig. 6: Snip the remaining slits straight across.

Fig. 7: Stretch the strip into yarn.

5. Slide a piece of cardboard into the tube with the uncut section running down the middle. Snip a diagonal cut at the bottom and then more diagonal cuts to connect the slit on the left to the next slit up on the right as shown (fig. 5).

6. Center the remaining uncut section on the cardboard, and snip the slits on the other side of the tee straight across (fig. 6). This will create a long, continuous strip of knit fabric.

7. Start at one end of the strip and begin stretching it so that it curls inward on itself, creating T-shirt "yarn" (fig. 7).

Fig. 8: Stack and stitch three pieces of yarn.

Fig. 9: Tape and braid the yarn.

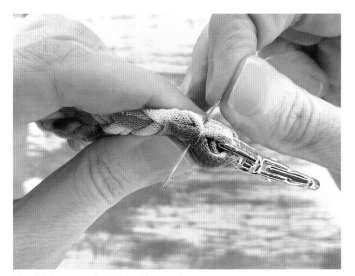

Fig. 10: Loop and stitch to the hardware.

Fig. 11: Wrap and finish.

8. Snip three lengths of yarn to about 40" (1 m). Uncurl the ends a bit and stack the three pieces, then stitch the ends to hold them together (fig. 8).

9. Use masking tape to anchor the yarn ends to the table. Braid the yarn, then stitch the bottom end the same way as the top (fig. 9).

10. Bring the two braid ends together and thread through the lanyard loop. Stitch to attach securely (fig. 10).

11. Wrap a bit of extra yarn around the stitched overlap to hide it. Stitch and glue the ends to finish (fig. 11).

MINI CROSS-STITCH
ZIPPER PULL

Cross-stitch is a timeless and classic craft. Both simple designs and incredibly intricate ones can be created by making the signature X-shaped stitches on aida cloth. The sky is the limit. In this beginner's project, brightly colored embroidery floss stitches are stacked to form a basic rainbow sequence. The result is oh-so satisfying and adorably "mini." A few extra steps with scissors and glue puts your handiwork on display as a stylish zipper pull for a favorite handbag or backpack. Perfection.

MATERIALS

- ☐ Paper
- ☐ Ruler or tape measure
- ☐ Pencil
- ☐ Scissors
- ☐ Rectangle pendant bezel (necklace pendant with a flat back and raised edges)
- ☐ Aida cloth (11 or 14 count)
- ☐ Small embroidery hoop
- ☐ Embroidery floss *(various colors)*
- ☐ Embroidery needles
- ☐ White glue
- ☐ Small clothespins
- ☐ Jump ring
- ☐ Swivel clasp

1. Measure and cut a paper template that fits inside your bezel (fig. 1). A little wiggle room is okay because the aida cloth's thickness will fill it out.

2. Stretch a piece of the aida cloth onto a small embroidery hoop. Trace the paper template onto the cloth to establish the borders for your cross-stitch design (fig. 2).

3. Cut about 24" (61 cm) of embroidery floss and divide it so you are working with only three strands (fig. 3). This will create less bulk for such a small design and bezel setting.

4. Choose a rainbow of colors you like for this striped design. Lay them out in the order you want to stitch them. Choose the center color and make your first row of stitches in the center of your design. Make a full row of diagonal stitches first. Come up from the back of the fabric through the corner of one of the woven squares in the aida cloth. Stitch back down through the diagonal corner of the same square. Then do the same across the row (fig. 4).

5. Stitch your way back across your first row but with diagonal stitches that "cross" the first set to make an X (fig. 5). Stitch two rows of each color as described in the previous steps. Tuck the floss tails into some of the stitches on the back to keep them secure each time you switch colors.

Fig. 1: Make a template.

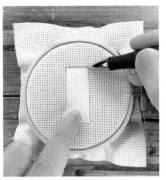

Fig. 2: Stretch the cloth and trace the template.

Fig. 3: Thin the embroidery floss.

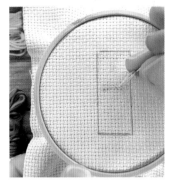

Fig. 4: Choose your colors and make the first row of diagonal stitches.

Fig. 5: Make the cross-stitches, or Xs. Continue stitching two rows of each color.

Fig. 6: Trim the finished design.

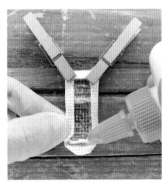

Fig. 7: Glue back the edges.

Fig. 8: Make the zipper pull.

6. When the design is complete, trim the fabric with a small border (about three rows) all around. Trim the corners at a 45-degree angle, being careful not to snip through the cloth too close to the corner threads (fig. 6).

7. Use a generous amount of white glue to fold back and secure the edges of your design (fig. 7). You can use small clothespins to keep the cloth in place while the glue dries.

8. Glue the completed cross-stitch design into the bezel and attach a jump ring and swivel clasp to finish (fig. 8).

NOW TRY THIS!

- Add your charm to a necklace, lanyard, or keychain if you prefer.

- You can spell words or names, or even make little illustrations in floss.

- Convert an image to pixels in a graphics program and use the pixel art as a cross-stitch pattern. Digital art meets handmade craft!

STRING ART
COLOR WHEEL

String art is an oldie but goodie craft that every kid should try at least once. After all, everyone should know how to hammer in a nail. And this project offers lots of practice! Wrapping the nails with brightly colored string turns what initially looks like a woodshop project into a true work of art. The resulting color wheel design is beautiful, textural, and lots of fun.

MATERIALS

☐ Round wood board, 18″ (46 cm) diameter shown here (choose a soft wood to make hammering easier—if you use a harder wood, you may want an adult to drill pilot holes at each of the marks to make it easier to drive in the nails)

☐ Pencil

☐ Ruler

☐ Cloth tape measure

☐ 1″ to 1.5″ (2.5 to 4 cm) flathead nails

☐ Hammer

☐ Embroidery floss, yarn, or other string (various colors)

☐ White glue

1. Make a dot at center of the wood circle. Divide the circle into wedges based on how many string colors you have. Draw lines through the center dot to make the wedge shapes (fig. 1). This example shows twelve colors, so the circle is divided into twelve wedges.

2. Use the cloth tape measure to mark evenly spaced dots all around the perimeter of the board (fig. 2). In this example, ½″ (1 cm) spaces are shown. Make the marks about ¼″ (6 mm) away from the edge of the wood.

3. Mark a pencil dot inside each wedge about 1″ (2.5 cm) away from the center (fig. 3). This will be the anchor nail for each color of string.

4. Hammer nails at every pencil mark, keeping the nail heads at about the same height as much as possible (fig. 4).

5. Lay out the colored string all around the edges of the circle (fig. 5). The color positions should match those on the color wheel, but don't worry about being too exact.

Fig. 1: Divide the wood circle into wedges (based on the number of string colors you have).

Fig. 2: Make pencil dots around the edges to mark nail positions.

Fig. 3: Mark a dot inside each wedge near the center.

Fig. 4: Hammer in the nails.

Fig. 5: Position the string around the circle.

Fig. 6: Knot the first string on the center nail and glue.

Fig. 7: Wrap the first string color from the center to the edges to create a wedge shape of string.

Fig. 8: Repeat wrapping with all other colors.

6. Knot the first color under the center nail head, trim the tail, and secure the knot with white glue (fig. 6).

7. Wrap the first color from the center toward the edge nails and back and forth in a figure-eight pattern until all the edge nails in that wedge are used (fig. 7). Tie off the tail end along the last edge nail and glue the knot. Repeat the wrapping with all the other colors until the wheel is complete (fig 8).

LITTLE HANDS

Younger kids will need adult help with nails. It's also a good idea to use a single, thick, variegated color yarn rather than many colors with knot tying. Consider pounding a random smattering of nails on a board for younger artists. Then they can simply zig-zag the string randomly from nail to nail to make any pattern they wish.

COLORFUL WHIRLIGIG

Some scrap cardboard plus a little paint and string can turn into a fun toy in no time. Whirligigs are old-school crafts that still pack a lot of fun. Try lots of different designs to see which create the best spin effects. Then challenge your friends to see who can get their whirligig spinning the longest.

MATERIALS

☐ Pencil

☐ Heavy scrap cardboard

☐ Art paper

☐ Scissors

☐ Paint or markers to decorate

☐ Glue stick

☐ Skewer

☐ Yarn or string

☐ Jingle bells *(optional)*

☐ Jewelry pliers *(optional)*

☐ Jump rings *(optional)*

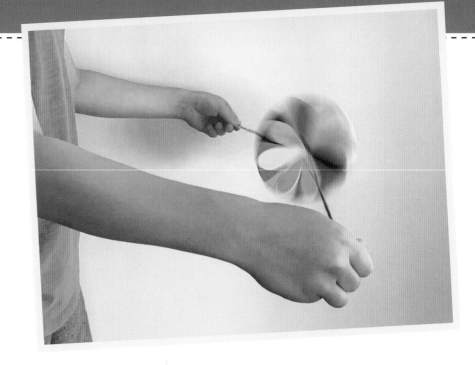

1. Trace a circle that is approximately 5″ to 6″ (13 to 15 cm) in diameter onto the heavy cardboard and two pieces of art paper (fig. 1). A small bowl makes a great template to trace.

2. Cut out the cardboard and paper circles (fig. 2).

3. Use paint or markers to make fun designs on each paper circle (fig. 3). Think about designs that will look interesting or beautiful while spinning.

4. Attach the paper circle designs to each side of the cardboard using a glue stick (fig. 4).

5. Use a skewer to poke holes near the center of the disc (fig. 5). The holes should be about ½″ (1 cm) from the center and aligned with one another.

6. Snip about 48″ (1.2 m) of yarn or string for the handles (fig. 6).

7. Thread the yarn or string through the holes in the disc and knot the ends to create a continuous loop (fig. 7).

8. If you like, poke holes around the edges of the disc and attach jingle bells using jewelry pliers and jump rings (fig. 8). This not only makes a fun sound, but it also adds a bit of weight to the disc that makes it easier to twirl.

Fig. 1: Trace circles onto cardboard and paper.

Fig. 2: Cut out the circles.

Fig. 3: Create designs on the paper circles.

Fig. 4: Glue the circles together.

Fig. 5: Poke holes in the center.

Fig. 6: Cut a length of string.

Fig. 7: Thread the string and knot.

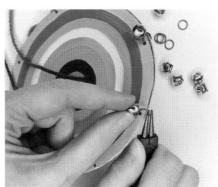

Fig. 8: Attach jingle bells.

DIRECTIONS FOR WHIRLIGIG PLAY

Stand holding the string loops in each hand with the disc centered and upright. Loosely begin to swing the disc in a circle to twist the strings. Once the strings are twisted, pull the strings outward sharply to force the strings to unwind and make the disc spin. It takes a little practice at first, but it's lots of fun once you get the hang of it!

PRESSED FLOWER STICKERS

Pressing and drying flowers is a wonderful way to preserve memories. You can save flowers from your first garden or from a bouquet you received for a special occasion. It can also be a beautiful way to create floral collage elements, craft decorations, and these precious homemade stickers. You can press the flowers in a hurry with your household iron instead of waiting days using a traditional flower press. Using just some clear shelf liner and packing tape, you can add a pretty bit of nature to envelopes, folders, notebooks, and more with these delicate little decals.

MATERIALS

☐ Small fresh flowers

☐ Parchment or typing paper

☐ Heavy books or bricks

☐ Iron

☐ Clear adhesive (or white) shelf liner

☐ Packing tape

☐ Scissors

LITTLE HANDS

Skip right to the sticker making by using premade dried flowers. Or have little ones make tiny pieces of artwork and turn those into stickers using this same method. Trace around a coin to give them a good-size border to draw within. Homemade crayon art stickers are adorable!

Fig. 1: Snip the flowers.

Fig. 2: Lay out the blooms on paper.

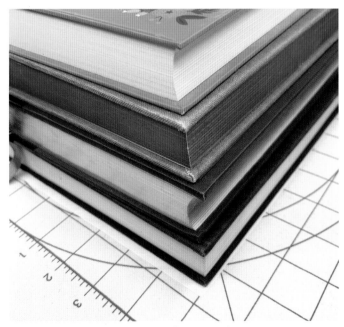

Fig. 3: Cover with another sheet of paper and press.

1. Choose some pretty blossoms and snip them off very close to the flower head (fig. 1).

2. Arrange the blooms onto parchment or typing paper (fig. 2). Give them plenty of room so they won't overlap other flowers when you press.

3. Carefully cover the flowers with another sheet of parchment or typing paper and stack heavy books on top to begin flattening the flowers (fig. 3). Leave this for at least 15 minutes, but the longer the better, even overnight!

(continued)

Fig. 4: Iron the flowers.

Fig. 5: Peel back the paper and remove the flowers.

Fig. 6: Arrange the flowers on shelf liner.

4. Use a *dry* household iron on the lowest possible setting to press the flowers between the sheets of paper (fig. 4). Be sure the iron is emptied of water. High heat and steam will brown the flowers. Press firmly no longer than 5 to 10 seconds in each location. Do not slide the iron. Pick it up and press one flower, then pick it up and move to another. Check the flowers intermittently to see if they are fully dried. They should not feel moist. Continue pressing until you achieve very dry blooms that feel delicate like tissue paper.

5. Carefully remove the top sheet of paper and remove the dried flowers (fig. 5). Be very gentle. Dried flowers are a bit brittle and can crumble.

6. Tape down a sheet of shelf liner shiny-side up and paper-backing-side down. Arrange your dried flowers on the sheet to make a set of stickers (fig. 6). You can use a single bloom or a little cluster. Just be sure your clusters are not larger than the width of the packing tape.

Fig. 7: Tape down the flowers.

Fig. 8: Trim the stickers.

Fig. 9: Peel and stick!

7. Rip off squares of packing tape and carefully cover each flower or cluster (fig. 7). Press down firmly to get a good seal all around the dried flowers. You should maintain about ¼" (6 mm) border of packing tape all the way around each flower or cluster to be sure the packing tape is securely adhered. Press out any air bubbles.

8. Use scissors to cut out each sticker (fig. 8). Don't trim too close to the flowers. Keep at least ¼" (6 mm) border to be sure there is a good seal.

9. To use the stickers, simply peel away the shelf liner paper backing (fig. 9)!

NOW TRY THIS!

Go one step further and make sticker strips to give to your friends! Cut a bit of waxed paper and tape it to a piece of cardboard. Stick a few stickers to the waxed paper. They will be removable for your friends to enjoy!

KANTHA CLOTH–INSPIRED
DRINK COZIES

Traditional *kantha* stitching is used to create thin cushions or scarves from layered Indian saris. This pretty drink cozy is inspired by those beautiful textiles. The layered fabric offers some insulation from a hot drink, plus a soft grip. The rows of running stitches are lovely to look at as well as fun and easy to practice. This is a great project for embroidery beginners. If you can master the simple stitches plus sewing on a button, you've got it made. The hardest part is choosing from all the beautiful floss colors!

MATERIALS

☐ Linen fabric (cotton is a good substitute)

☐ Straight pins

☐ Cardboard drink sleeve (to use as a template)

☐ Pencil

☐ Scissors

☐ Thin elastic band (about 3" [7.5 cm])

☐ Embroidery floss (seven or eight colors)

☐ Embroidery needle

☐ Button

LITTLE HANDS

Have younger kids do slightly larger stitches and fewer rows to make this project more attainable. An adult can stitch the edges together first and let the kids make the rows of running stitches to avoid prickly pins or the possibility of fabric becoming misaligned in the process.

1. Pin three layers of linen together (you may want four or five layers if it is very thin). Carefully open up a cardboard sleeve from your local coffee shop. Trace it on the fabric with an extra ½" (6 mm) all around (fig. 1).

2. Cut through all three layers of fabric so that you have three same-size stacked pieces (fig. 2).

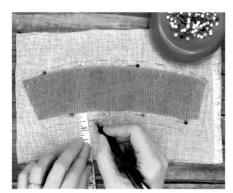

Fig. 1: Trace the template.

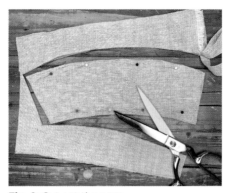

Fig. 2: Cut out the cozy.

Fig. 3: Sew the elastic loop.

Fig. 4: Reposition the pins and choose the floss colors.

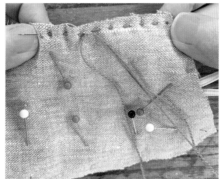

Fig. 5: Make the rows of stitching.

Fig. 6: Add the button.

3. Loop about 3″ (7.5 cm) of thin elastic and sew the ends between two of the layers of fabric on the short end (fig. 3). The ends will be sandwiched between the layers and secured even further by all the rows of stitches you'll be making.

4. Remove the few pins you were using and replace them with more pins about every inch (2.5 cm) or so perpendicular to the cut edges, points facing outward (fig. 4). This will help hold the layers together and in alignment as you begin stitching. You can remove them as you go, once the stitches begin doing the job.

5. Thread your needle and knot the end. Make a row of small, even stitches very close to the top edge (fig. 5). You can push the needle in and out of the fabric several times before pulling through to make three or four stitches at once. This also helps to keep the rows fairly straight and in line. Continue with all the colors, doing as many rows of each color as you like until you reach the bottom edge. Simple knots on the back are fine as you finish with each color.

6. Try your cozy on a cup to mark the position of the button and stitch it in place (fig. 6). Knot the tails securely on the back.

NOW TRY THIS!

- Try different fabrics on the front and back of the cozy to make it reversible. Use hook-and-loop closures instead of a button to make this idea work!

- Use interesting fabrics like old silk scarves to make this project even more authentic to the *kantha* inspiration.

UNIT
6

15-Minute Makes

If you've been neglecting your craftiness because of a jam-packed schedule, you're in luck. This little selection of crafts is low mess and high impact and requires minimal time commitment. If you have about 15 minutes, you can complete a craft. Younger kids may need a little more time, but you'll still be showing off your handiwork in a flash. Make a fringy keychain and walk right out the door with it! Snip up a T-shirt, tie some knots, and be off to visit a friend. Make a whole handful of paper-clip bookmarks and still have plenty of time to read a dozen chapters. Not every creative pursuit needs to book a four-hour slot in your life. Everybody can find a little time to feed their creativity.

EASY FRINGED LEATHER KEYRING

These easy keyrings are effortlessly cool and can be worked up in a flash. The completed keyrings are great for your house key, but they also make a cute zipper pull on your backpack or a thoughtful gift for your mom, dad, or favorite teacher.

MATERIALS

☐ Soft leather

☐ Ruler or tape measure

☐ Scissors

☐ Keyring

☐ Embroidery floss

☐ Sewing needle

☐ White glue

1. Cut a strip of leather measuring 1″ × 5″ (2.5 × 12.5 cm) (fig. 1).

2. Fold the strip in half with the keyring tucked into the crease (fig. 2).

3. Thread a needle with floss and tie a knot. Start your first stitch from the inside edge of the leather so the knot is hidden (fig. 3).

4. Create three neat stitches through both layers of leather close to the keyring (fig. 4). Repeat on the opposite side.

5. Use your needle to twist the tail of thread around the existing section between the layers of leather (fig. 5).

6. Make a knot and trim the floss (fig. 6).

7. Dab a little white glue on the knot to secure it (fig. 7).

8. Use sharp scissors to cut narrow fringe into the leather (fig. 8). Leave about ¼″ (6 mm) between the fringe and stitching.

LITTLE HANDS

Younger kids may have a hard time pushing the needle through the leather. Try some other softer non-fraying fabrics or faux leather or suede to make it easier on their hands, or encourage the use of a thimble. Just be sure to keep safety in mind. Needles should always be pushed away from the face and body so that nobody gets pricked.

Fig. 1: Cut a leather strip.

Fig. 2: Fold the leather through the keyring.

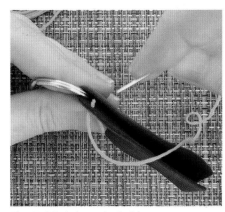

Fig. 3: Stitch from the inside.

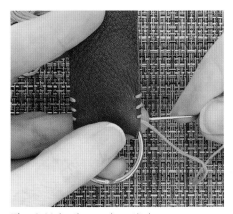

Fig. 4: Make three edge stitches on each side.

Fig. 5: Secure the thread between the layers.

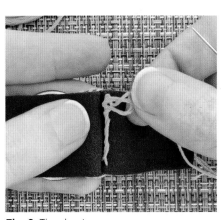

Fig. 6: Tie a knot.

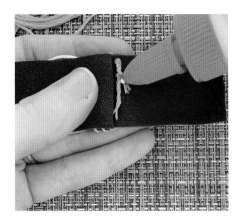

Fig. 7: Glue the knot.

Fig. 8: Cut the fringe.

NOW TRY THIS!

Experiment with stitching patterns to change things up. Try a running stitch or a row of vertical stitches. Use your creativity! Add a stretchy beaded bracelet to the keyring to make it hands free and high fashion!

T-SHIRT TOTE BAGS

This project is an oldie but goodie because it combines three major factors of a great craft. It upcycles materials you already have on hand, so it's good for the planet. It works up quickly. And it yields something truly useful (and stylish). It's the feel-good craft for everybody! Just find some old tees and get busy snipping!

MATERIALS

☐ T-shirt

☐ Scissors

☐ Masking tape

☐ Pen

☐ Tape measure or ruler

1. Lay your tee flat and carefully cut off the collar and sleeves (fig. 1). Try to cut a little bit away from the seams to be sure you remove them completely and leave the cut edge as smooth as you can, without jagged bits. If you start with a tank top, you can skip the sleeve and neckline cutting. Just start at step 2 and continue!

2. Cut off the bottom hem of the tee (fig. 2). If your shirt has a high-low hemline (as shown), just cut a straight line across at the shortest point.

3. Place a piece of masking tape across the shirt about 6" (15 cm) away from the bottom edge (fig. 3).

4. Make a cutting guide on the masking tape by marking every ½" (1 cm) with a pen (fig. 4).

5. Make a cut at every ½" (1 cm) mark through both layers of the tee, up to the masking tape (fig. 5).

Fig. 1: Cut off the collar and sleeves.

Fig. 2: Trim off the bottom hem.

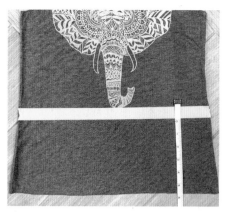

Fig. 3: Mark 6″ (15 cm) with masking tape.

Fig. 4: Mark the tape every ½″ (1 cm).

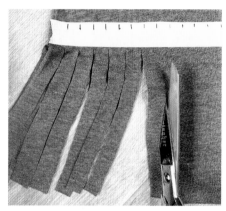

Fig. 5: Cut the fringe.

Fig. 6: Double knot the fringe.

Fig. 7: Make adjustments.

6. Working left to right, separate each front fringe from its back fringe partner and tie in a double knot right up to the tape (fig. 6). Then remove the tape.

7. Tighten the knots to secure the bag bottom, and fluff the fringe as necessary (fig. 7).

NOW TRY THIS!

- If you prefer to have a bag without fringe, turn your tee inside out before you begin. When finished, trim the fringe off and turn the bag right side out so that remaining knot tails are on the inside of the bag.

ARTSY DESKTOP
DRY ERASE BOARD

Chores and checklists never looked this good! Make this colorful desktop dry erase board to keep track of your practice schedule, homework assignments, and weekend plans. Then just swipe with a tissue and start fresh again. It's a great way to repurpose an old picture frame into something useful and stylish. So break out your paints and brushes. It's the start of the new organized YOU!

MATERIALS

☐ Desktop picture frame (about 8" × 10" [20 × 25 cm] works well)

☐ Craft paints (various colors)

☐ Paintbrush

☐ Pencil

☐ Scrapbook paper or wrapping paper with a light pattern

☐ Dry erase marker

☐ Colorful duct tape (optional)

☐ Self-adhesive hook-and-loop tape

1. Remove the glass from the frame and paint the frame using bright colors and layered vertical brush strokes (fig. 1). Keep adding strokes until the entire frame is covered. Then add a few dot clusters for extra movement.

2. Trace the frame's cardboard insert or glass onto lightly patterned scrapbook paper or wrapping paper (fig. 2). This will give some style to the background of your dry erase board, without making your writing too tough to read.

3. Use scissors to cut the paper background to size (fig. 3).

4. Place the trimmed background paper into the frame under the glass (fig. 4).

5. Use colorful duct tape to wrap the dry erase marker so it coordinates with the painted frame (fig. 5). This step is optional, but it really makes the project look complete!

Fig. 1: Paint the frame.

Fig. 2: Trace the frame insert.

Fig. 3: Cut the paper.

Fig. 4: Insert the background paper.

Fig. 5: Duct tape the marker.

Fig. 6: Stick the hook-and-loop tape to the marker.

Fig. 7: Stick the hook-and-loop tape to the frame.

6. Peel and stick the soft side of the hook-and-loop tape to the side of the marker (fig. 6). The hard hook side won't be as comfy while you are writing.

7. Peel and stick the hard side of the hook and loop tape to the side of the frame (fig. 7).

NOW TRY THIS!

- Use a weekly or monthly blank calendar as the background insert for an easy dry erase calendar.

- Use your board to write ever-changing inspirational quotes or positive affirmations right where you can see them every day.

Calling all athletes! Team-issued uni-
forms are often one-size-fits-all and
need a little intervention to be more
comfy and breezy. These super-simple
bands convert baggy short-sleeved
jerseys to a sleeveless option in a
flash. Using different ribbon for front
and back even makes them reversible!
Match them to your uniform or coordinate them to your sport. They come
together so quickly, you could make
them for your whole team in no time!

MATERIALS

☐ 2 types of 1″ (2.5 cm)-wide
   grosgrain ribbon

☐ Iron

☐ 1″ (2.5 cm)-wide fusible bonding tape

☐ Hook-and-loop tape

☐ Needle and thread

1. Cut four strips of ribbon (two of each design) to about 6″ (15 cm) long (fig. 1). You can adjust this length a bit to suit your own size.

2. Use a warm iron to press the ends of your ribbon under about ¼″ (6 mm) (fig. 2). This will keep the edges from fraying on your finished scruncher.

3. Cut one piece of fusible bonding tape for each scruncher (fig. 3). It should be exactly to length without protruding. (The iron will stick to it if the two touch.)

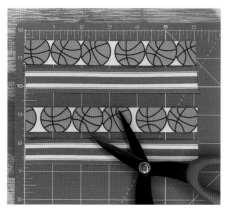

Fig. 1: Cut the ribbon.

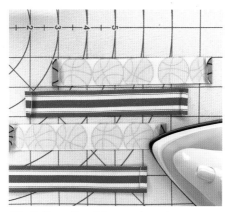

Fig. 2: Press the ribbon ends under.

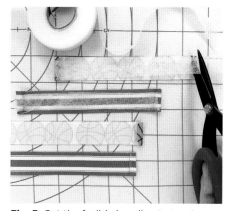

Fig. 3: Cut the fusible bonding tape to length.

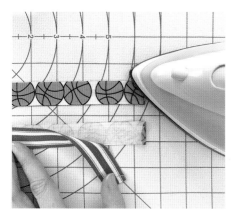

Fig. 4: Fuse the ribbons.

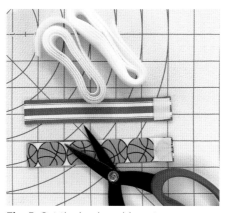

Fig. 5: Cut the hook-and-loop tape.

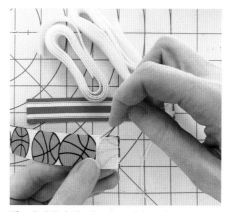

Fig. 6: Stitch the hook-and-loop tape.

4. Sandwich the fusible bonding tape between lengths of ribbon (fig. 4). Place your first ribbon design on the bottom and the second ribbon design on top. Press to fuse. Repeat for the second set of ribbons.

5. Snip hook-and-loop tape to fit across the end of the ribbon (fig. 5).

6. Stitch the hook-and-loop tape to the ends of the scrunchers so they make a loop when connected (fig. 6). For example, the soft loop side will go on the first ribbon design, and the hard hook side will go on the second ribbon design on the opposite end.

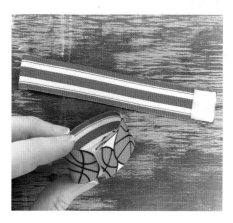

PAPERCLIP BOOKMARKS

Here's a craft you can make in a hurry and use right away while doing your reading homework. The common thread in these cute paperclip bookmarks is the string or ribbon looped through the end of the clip. Simple. But adding cute touches like pompoms and feathers or using multiple strands of yarn for a tassel effect is where your creativity comes in. So raid the junk drawer and craft cabinet for inspiration. You'll have enough ideas to make a whole set!

MATERIALS

☐ String

☐ Ruler or tape measure

☐ Scissors

☐ Jumbo paperclips

☐ White glue

☐ Mini pompoms

1. Snip three strands of string to about 8" (20 cm) each (fig. 1).

2. Fold the bunch of string in half and thread it through the end of the paperclip (fig. 2).

3. Bring the tails of the string over the paperclip and through the loop (fig. 3). Pull to tighten. It helps to secure the tightened knot with a dab of glue.

4. Trim the six strings to different lengths so your pompoms will be staggered (fig. 4).

5. Push back the pompom fluff to find the center/knot and dab on a bit of white glue (fig. 5).

6. Place the end of one of the trimmed strings into the dot of glue. Hold it in place a few seconds and then fluff the pompom back up around the string (fig. 6).

7. Repeat step 6 for all the strings until you have a full pompom tassel on the paperclip (fig. 7).

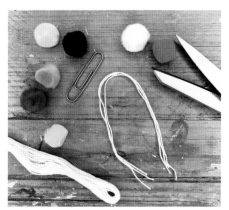

Fig. 1: Cut the string.

Fig. 2: Fold and insert the string.

Fig. 3: Pull the tails through the loop.

Fig. 4: Trim the strings.

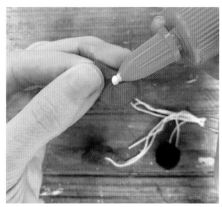

Fig. 5: Put a dot of glue in the pompom.

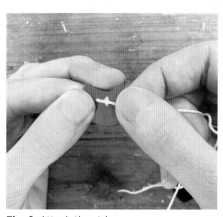

Fig. 6: Attach the string.

Fig. 7: Glue all the pompoms on.

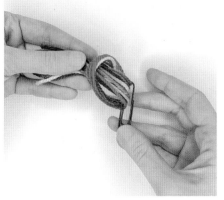

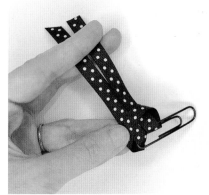

The looping technique can be used to make the yarn tassel bookmark and ribbon bookmark.

PHOTO GALLERY
PINBOARD

Friends and family are what it's all about. Make this quick and easy photo pinboard from used shipping boxes, plus some fabric and string. Then add cute little clothespins and push pins for two ways to attach your memories. It's perfect to hang on your wall or prop on a shelf or desk. Choose fabric to coordinate with your room or use school colors for a "team memories" board you'll love.

MATERIALS

- ☐ 4 pieces of corrugated cardboard the same size *(12″ × 16″ [30 × 40 cm] or larger is recommended)*
- ☐ Scissors
- ☐ Masking tape
- ☐ Thin cotton fabric *(large enough to wrap around your chosen cardboard size)*
- ☐ String or twine
- ☐ Pushpins
- ☐ Mini clothespins

1. Cut rectangles of corrugated cardboard into four equal-size rectangles (fig. 1).

2. Stack the cardboard rectangles and use masking tape to wrap around each of the four sides to hold it together (fig 2).

3. Place the cardboard onto the fabric and wrap it around the edges to the back and tape down (fig. 3). Tuck the corners as though you were wrapping a gift. Press firmly on the masking tape. Warming the adhesive with your hand and applying pressure will make it stick with no problem.

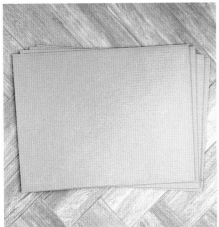
Fig. 1: Cut the cardboard.

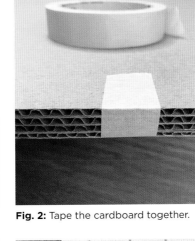
Fig. 2: Tape the cardboard together.

Fig. 3: Wrap the fabric.

Fig. 4: Add a string at the top of the board.

Fig. 5: Add a string at the bottom of the board.

Fig. 6: Add mini clothespins and pushpins.

4. Insert a pushpin into the board near the top left and another at top right. Cut a length of string a little wider than the board. Tie a knot around the push pin at top left and then another at top right so that you have a little clothesline across the top of the board (fig. 4).

5. Follow the same steps to make a little clothesline at the bottom of the board (fig. 5).

6. Clip some mini clothespins to the strings and add some cute pushpins to the board (fig. 6). Add a few favorite photos, ribbons, and special mementos to get your display started.

EXTRA HELP

Cutting large pieces of cardboard can be difficult. Enlist the help of an adult if any dangerous cutting tool is necessary.

GUITAR PICK
NECKLACE

These cool guitar pick necklaces are fun to make and easily adaptable for all ages. It's the perfect craft for any budding musician or music lover. Find unique guitar picks to use for this project in music shops or online. Trade them like marbles with your friends. Even customize pick designs using craft paint and other craft supplies.

MATERIALS

☐ Guitar picks

☐ Masking tape

☐ Scrap wood

☐ Hammer

☐ Small, slim nail

☐ Jewelry pliers

☐ Jump rings

☐ Leather cord

☐ Necklace hardware

LITTLE HANDS

Younger kids may wish to skip the jewelry hardware and simply tie a knot in a longer cord for a necklace that slips over their head.

1. Use masking tape to secure the pick to a piece of scrap wood (fig. 1). This will help keep the pick from shifting during step 2.

2. Use a hammer and slim nail to gently tap a hole into your pick (fig. 2). Just tap the point in, not the thickest part of the nail, or it may crack.

Fig. 1: Tape the pick to scrap wood.

Fig. 2: Make a hole.

Fig. 3: Attach the jump ring.

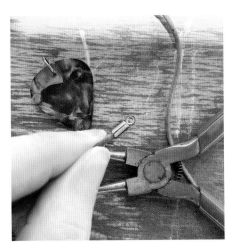
Fig. 4: Attach end caps to the cord.

Fig. 5: Attach jump rings.

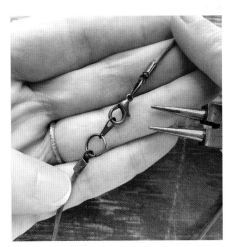
Fig. 6: Attach the closure.

3. Use jewelry pliers to open a large jump ring and thread the pick onto it (fig. 3). Close the ring. You have a charm!

4. Snip a length of leather cord sized for your neck. Crimp jewelry end caps with small eyes onto both ends of the leather cord (fig. 4).

5. Use jewelry pliers to attach more jump rings as connectors between the end caps and the necklace closure (fig. 5).

6. Attach a lobster clasp or other necklace closure to complete the necklace (fig. 6).

NOW TRY THIS!

Decorate your guitar pick with craft paint, gemstones, and stickers to make it your own. Trade guitar pick charms with friends and start a mini collection.

Crafting with Kindness

Wouldn't it be great if an afternoon of creativity made someone else as happy as it made you? It can! You can craft all sorts of things to share with others when they need them most. Make pet blankets for your local animal shelter. Assemble lollipop flowers to share with your friends after a swim meet. Collect spare change in a clever, homemade donations jar and deliver it to a favorite charity. Even paint words of encouragement and positivity onto rocks you scatter throughout your community to brighten the day of anyone who passes by. When your focus is outward, rather than inward, there is no end to the imaginative ways you will find to pay your blessings forward in kindness.

NO-SEW FRINGED
PET BLANKETS

Spend an afternoon with a friend making this sweet and cozy pet blanket. Non-fraying fleece and the simple knotted fringe technique make this craft easy to do with very few supplies. Donate your completed blanket to a local animal shelter to spread a bit of kindness to some furry friends. It will make their day and yours.

MATERIALS

☐ 2 pieces of fleece (*measuring about 40" × 40" [1 × 1 m]*)

☐ Tape measure

☐ Scissors

☐ Straight pins

☐ Masking tape

☐ Pen

1. Measure, cut, and align two 40" × 40" (1 × 1 m) pieces of fleece (fig. 1).

2. Measure a 6" (15 cm) square in each corner and mark it with pins. Cut and remove the 6" (15 cm) squares from each corner (fig. 2).

3. Place long strips of masking tape along each edge, 6" (15 cm) away from each edge, to create a cutting guide for the fringe (fig. 3).

4. Measure and mark the tape guides at 1" (2.5 cm) intervals as a guide to keep the fringe width uniform (fig. 4).

5. Cut 1" (2.5 cm) strips of fringe along each blanket edge, stopping at the tape (fig. 5). Cut through both layers of fleece and use the 1" (2.5 cm) markings as a guide for width.

6. Tie front to back by knotting each fringe "stack" as you would tie a balloon. Make a loop (fig. 6), pull both tails through the loop (fig. 7), and slide the knot up to the tape (fig. 8). Repeat around all sides of the blanket.

Fig. 1: Cut the fleece squares.

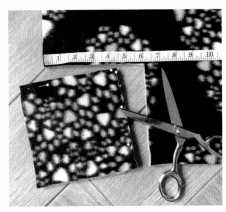

Fig. 2: Cut out the corners.

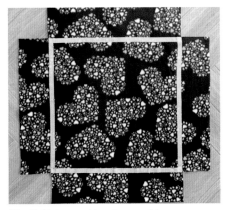

Fig. 3: Make masking-tape guides.

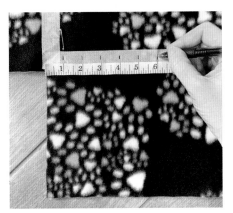

Fig. 4: Mark off the cuts.

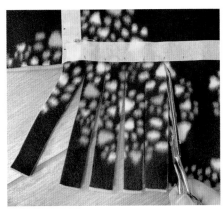

Fig. 5: Snip the fringe.

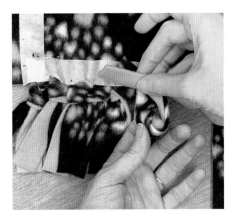

Fig. 6: Make a loop.

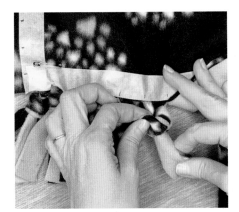

Fig. 7: Pull both tails through the loop.

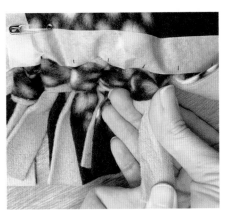

Fig. 8: Slide the knot up to the tape.

LITTLE HANDS

Younger kids may not have the dexterity to tie this type of knot neatly. A little teamwork may be in order. Perhaps an adult can make the loop and allow the child to pull the ends through. Or an adult or older child can tie the knots while a younger kiddo can fluff the fringe as they go.

AIR PLANT BUDDIES

Air plants are great for kids! They require very little care; just a spritz of water once a week will keep them thriving. They don't even require potting soil. In this project, the spiky, grassy, wavy air plants act as "hair" for our little buddies! An adorable small pot is painted as the face, complete with google eyes for fun! If you'd like, you can add small bead "feet" to give your pal even more charm. Use your imagination to create a whole squad of green-haired friends!

MATERIALS

☐ Small terracotta pots (or any small pot you can decorate)

☐ Craft paint (various colors)

☐ Small paintbrushes

☐ Googly eyes

☐ White glue

☐ Spanish moss or other fill for pots

☐ Air plants

☐ Hot glue gun (optional)

☐ Small wooden beads (optional)

1. Paint your pot with a base layer of craft paint (fig. 1). Be sure to paint about 1″ (2.5 cm) or more down inside the pot as well so it doesn't look messy once the plant is inside. Leave the bottom unpainted. Paint several pots if you want to make an air plant family!

2. Paint a face onto a painted pot with a small paintbrush (fig. 2). It may be helpful to mark the eyes with dots at this stage.

3. Glue googly eyes onto the pot with white glue (fig. 3).

Fig. 1: Paint the flower pot a base color.

Fig. 2: Paint a face onto the pot.

Fig. 3: Glue on some googly eyes.

Fig. 4: Add moss and your air plant.

Fig. 5: Add feet to the pot.

4. Wrap a bit of Spanish moss around the base of the air plant and tuck it into the pot (fig. 4). No soil is required.

5. Hot glue wooden beads to the bottom of the pot in a triangle formation to act as feet, if you like (fig. 5).

LITTLE HANDS

Small children may find it easier to add faces with acrylic paint pens rather than paintbrushes. You can find these at most craft stores now. Permanent markers will work in a pinch.

PAINTED POSITIVITY PEBBLES

Here's a quick, simple, and colorful way to spread good vibes out into the world. Paint some words of encouragement and positivity onto found rocks. Decorate them with rows of vibrant dots to catch the eye. Then tuck them alongside walking paths in the park or amongst the flowers in your community garden. When folks passing by notice these unexpected little gems, they'll feel the warm fuzzies, and smiles will start spreading across their faces.

MATERIALS

☐ Rocks *(about 3" to 5" [7 to 13 cm] across)*

☐ Craft paints *(various colors)*

☐ Washable markers

☐ Paintbrushes

☐ Sealer or varnish

1. Paint a solid color onto each rock (fig 1). You may need a few coats. Be patient and allow each coat to dry before adding the next.

2. Use washable markers to write words onto the rocks (fig. 2). These will wipe off with a damp cloth if you make a mistake or want to make an adjustment to get the size and spacing just right. Choose empowering and positive words or short phrases that you will be able to paint easily.

3. Use a small detail brush to paint over the sketched words (fig. 3). Once dry, you can wipe off any marker that is still visible.

Fig. 1: Paint the base color.

Fig. 2: Sketch the words.

Fig. 3: Paint the words.

Fig. 4: Choose a pattern and make the first set of dots.

Fig. 5: Add dots in two additional colors.

Fig. 6: Add the finishing touches and sealer.

4. Choose a simple pattern and use the bottom end of your paintbrush to make perfect dots on the pebble. Dunk the bottom end in paint and dab it onto the rock (fig. 4). On the green rock shown, a radiating burst of dotted lines shines outward from the word. Start with vertical and horizontal rows of dots. Then add diagonal rows between those. Note that a circle pattern is used on the pink rock and arches of dots are used on the blue one. Repetition of the shapes is what makes the finished art look so striking. It's a simple but effective technique.

5. Continue to fill the spaces on the rock with more rows of dots in two more colors until the pebble looks well covered and complete (fig. 5).

6. Add any touches you'd like to finish your masterpiece. Then paint a clear sealer onto the rock to protect your work from the weather (fig. 6).

LITTLE HANDS

Younger kiddos can paint positive icons like smiley faces, hearts, and flowers onto their pebbles if words and dots prove too challenging. These precious symbol pebbles actually make for a beautiful little grouping when placed alongside a larger word rock.

CHEERFUL NOISE GUMBALL
TAMBOURINE

Want to brighten someone's day with a random act of kindness? Give them one of these smile-inducing treat tambourines filled with a rainbow of gumballs! After all, it's scientifically impossible to frown when you're blowing bubbles and shaking a tambourine! Decorate two paper plates with folksy sunshine and flowers. Stuff with gumballs or any favorite candies that make a great rattle. Pull it all together with pretty ribbon lacing and some streamers for fun. Who wouldn't appreciate such an unexpected gift of whimsy and joy?

MATERIALS

☐ 2 small paper plates (*dessert size*)

☐ Craft paints (*various colors*)

☐ Paintbrushes

☐ Painter's tape

☐ Hole punch

☐ Ruler or tape measure

☐ Plastic yarn needle

☐ 1″ (2.5 cm)-wide ribbon

☐ Gumballs or similar candies

☐ Mylar streamers, tinsel, or sparkly ribbon (*optional*)

1. Paint a cheerful design on the paper plates (fig. 1). A sunshine surrounded by folksy flowers is perfect. Start in the center and work your way outward.

2. Use painter's tape to hold the plates together and aligned as you punch holes around the edges (fig. 2). Match the spacing to about the same width as your selected ribbon. For 1″ (2.5 cm)-wide ribbon, 1″ (2.5 cm) spacing works well.

3. Thread a plastic yarn needle with the ribbon (fig. 3). This makes for easier lacing. If you don't have a yarn needle, you can roll the end of the ribbon tightly and tape it into a tube (like the end of a shoelace) to aid in lacing.

4. Leave a long tail, about 15″ (38 cm), and lace the plates together (fig. 4). Come up through the bottom of each hole. This will wrap the ribbon around the edges as you go. Stop lacing when there are two or three holes left. Don't forget to remove the tape as you go!

Fig. 1: Paint the plates.

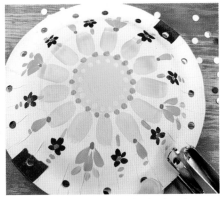
Fig. 2: Tape and punch holes in the plates.

Fig. 3: Thread the needle.

Fig. 4: Lace the plates together.

Fig. 5: Add the gumballs.

Fig. 6: Finish lacing and tie a bow.

Fig. 7: Add some sparkle!

5. Fill the tambourine with a couple handfuls of gumballs (fig. 5). You want to leave plenty of room for them to rattle around in there!

6. Complete the lacing and tie a nice bow with two long tails (fig. 6).

7. Loop some Mylar streamers, tinsel, or sparkly ribbon through one of the holes under the bow and pull tight, if you like (fig. 7).

NOW TRY THIS!

- Paint some excited, smiling, or laughing emojis on the paper plates to brighten someone's mood.

- Use one of these tambourines in place of a birthday card to top a wrapped gift. Write your message on the plate. It's a toy, a treat, and a gift tag in one!

LOLLIPOP BLOOMS

Make these adorable lollipop blooms to give to friends, neighbors, or anyone who looks like they could use a smile. Party streamers, tissue paper, and floral tape transform everyday candy into the ultimate sweet treat. Make a whole bagful for teammates after the soccer game or volunteers at the bake sale. Kindness breeds more kindness, so keep the good vibes going!

MATERIALS

☐ Fun tissue paper

☐ Crepe paper *(three colors)*

☐ Ruler or tape measure

☐ Scissors

☐ Lollipops

☐ Floral tape

☐ White glue

Teachable Moment

Cutting fringe and scallops is repetitious. Make the job easier, faster, and more even by folding the streamers in eighths. Then cut through *all* the layers to make fringe or petals. Unfold the streamers and see your perfectly cut petals and fringe in a fraction of the time.

1. Cut a 5″ (12.5 cm) square of your fun tissue, a 12″ (30.5 cm) piece of the crepe paper for the flower petals, and an 8″ (20 cm) piece of another crepe paper for the stamen/fringe (fig. 1). These sizes may vary for you depending on the type of lollipop you use. It's fine to estimate and make adjustments.

2. Cut the petal crepe paper into scallops and the stamen crepe paper into fringe (fig. 2). See the Teachable Moment sidebar for tips.

3. Wrap the fun tissue square over the lollipop and secure it to the stick with floral tape (fig. 3). Floral tape is stickier as you stretch it, so stretch as you wrap!

4. Squeeze a thin bead of glue along the edge of the streamer you snipped into fringe for the stamen (fig. 4).

5. Wrap the lollipop stick with the fringe (fig. 5). Pinch and press the glued edge into place as you wrap until it feels secure.

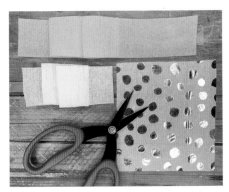

Fig. 1: Cut the tissue and streamers to size.

Fig. 2: Cut the streamers to shape.

Fig. 3: Cover the lollipop with tissue.

Fig. 4: Apply glue to the stamen fringe.

Fig. 5: Wrap the stamen.

Fig. 6: Glue and wrap the petals.

Fig. 7: Cut the leaves.

Fig. 8: Add the leaves with floral tape.

6. After applying a bead of glue, wrap the lollipop stick with the petals. Pinch and pleat as needed to make it look pretty (fig. 6). Then hold for a second or two until it feels secure.

7. Cut leaves from the third crepe paper color (fig. 7). Longer, slimmer leaves will be easiest to wrap into the floral tape.

8. Begin wrapping the base of the flower with floral tape, stretching the tape as you go to activate the adhesive. Tuck the leaves into the tape as you go (fig. 8). Continue wrapping until the stick is fully covered.

APPLE BACKYARD
BIRDFEEDER

Kindness extends to your backyard friends with this sweet birdfeeder project. Encourage some feathered visitors with just an apple, peanut butter, birdseed, and simple craft supplies. Colorful beads make these snacks as pretty as they are tasty. Just be sure to work outside on a nice day, and have napkins at the ready. This one gets a little sticky!

MATERIALS

☐ Stainless-steel straw or apple corer

☐ Apple

☐ String

☐ Wood beads

☐ Peanut butter

☐ Butter knife

☐ Paper plate

☐ Birdseed

☐ Skewers

☐ Scissors

1. Use a stainless-steel straw or an apple corer to make a hole through the center of the apple (fig. 1). A straw makes a smaller hole, which is ideal for anchoring the string hanger with beads. The bigger the hole, the larger your anchor bead will need to be.

2. Make a hanger for your birdfeeder by threading some string through the apple and tying beads at the tail end (fig. 2). Thread through a large bead first, then tie the string in a knot around a smaller bead and trim.

3. Use a butter knife to spread an even layer of peanut butter all over the apple (fig. 3). Make it just thick enough to grab the seed but not so thick that it is mushy when you handle it. This part gets messy. That's okay! You can wash up later.

4. Pour some birdseed onto a paper plate and rest the apple in it. Sprinkle and press seed into all areas of the peanut butter until the apple is well coated (fig. 4).

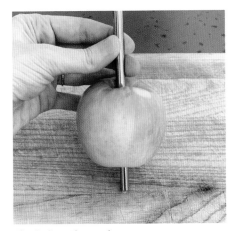
Fig. 1: Core the apple.

Fig. 2: Thread and anchor the string.

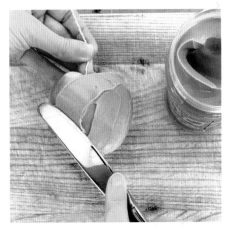
Fig. 3: Spread the peanut butter.

Fig. 4: Sprinkle on the birdseed.

Fig. 5: Insert the skewers.

Fig. 6: Snip off the skewer points.

5. The birds will appreciate a place to perch while they snack. Push two skewers through the center of the apple in an X (fig. 5). It can help to push through firmly one time, which will get the skewer about halfway through, then remove and push through another time to get the skewer all the way through. Always push away from your body and other people. Get an adult to help with this part to be on the safe side.

6. Use scissors to cut off the sharp ends of the skewers (fig. 6). Add a few more beads to the top part of the string hanger and tie it to the perfect tree.

EXTRA HELP

- Be sure to have an adult handy to help place the sharp skewers.

- Use sunflower seed butter if you have a peanut allergy.

WHEEL OF KINDNESS
SPINNER

Kindness should be a habit. Start each morning with a spin on this sweet wheel. Then be intentional during the day to follow the suggestion offered. This wheel reminds you to smile at those you meet, offer a hug to a friend, share a treat with someone who needs a lift, or donate to a worthy cause. Simple supplies make the board, and a repurposed fidget spinner makes it twirly fun! It's a great way to be more mindful about spreading care and kindness into the world around us.

MATERIALS

☐ Round objects for tracing *(such as a dinner plate and a ribbon spool)*

☐ Pencil

☐ Sturdy chipboard or cardboard

☐ Fidget spinner

☐ Ruler

☐ Scissors

☐ Foam double-stick tape

☐ Craft paints *(various colors)*

☐ Paintbrushes

☐ Paint marker

☐ Cotton swabs

1. Use a dinner plate or similar round object to trace a large circle onto a square piece of chipboard or cardboard (fig. 1).

2. Use a ribbon spool, jar lid, or other small round object to trace a smaller circle in the center of the large circle (fig. 2).

3. Use a ruler to draw a triangle around the fidget spinner on a separate piece of cardboard (fig. 3). The triangle should be a bit larger to completely cover the spinner when it is attached. Cut out the triangle.

4. Use a stack of foam tape on each corner to attach the spinner to the triangle (fig. 4). The stacks will allow the triangle to clear the center circle of the spinner.

5. Divide the circle into quadrants and paint a background color of craft paint onto each (fig. 5). Paint the triangle with a background color and a heart. The point of the heart is the pointer of the spinner.

Fig. 1: Trace a large circle.

Fig. 2: Trace a small circle.

Fig. 3: Draw a triangle around the fidget spinner and cut it out.

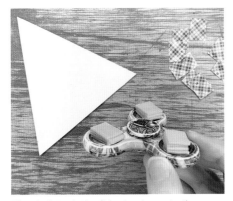

Fig. 4: Attach the fidget spinner to the triangle.

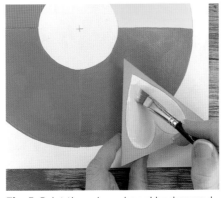

Fig. 5: Paint the spinner board background and the triangle.

Fig. 6: Paint the icons.

Fig. 7: Add double-stick foam tape to the center of the fidget spinner. Stick the spinner to the board.

6. Draw an icon onto each quadrant with paint marker and fill in with craft paint (fig. 6). Each icon symbolizes a way to be kind in the world. Use these examples or come up with your own. You can even use words if you like. Go ahead and embellish the rest of the board with paint now too. Paint the center circle and the board corners. Add dots with a cotton swab to bring everything to life.

7. Peel and stick two layers of foam tape to the center of the fidget spinner). Carefully align the spinner and stick. Take your time with this step because if the spinner is not placed directly in the center, the spin will seem off kilter. It can help to place it down a few times without the backing peeled off to check for centeredness. Then stick when you are confident (fig. 7).

"FULL HEART" DONATIONS JAR

Sharing is caring. And saving up coins to share is both kind and fun when you can use this cute craft project. Transform a mason jar into a perfectly sized donation spot with a little chalk paint and slotted cardboard on top. Leaving a window of clear glass lets you track your progress. Watch the coins pile higher and higher. When the heart is full, it's time to choose your favorite local charity and share the love. Then fill it up all over again.

MATERIALS

☐ Paper

☐ Scissors

☐ Masking tape

☐ Waxed paper

☐ Pencil

☐ Mason jar

☐ Chalk paint

☐ Paintbrush

☐ Toothpick

☐ Glitter puffy paint

☐ Scrap of cardboard (an empty cereal box is the perfect weight)

1. Cut a paper heart the right size for your mason jar (fig. 1).

2. Overlap strips of masking tape on a piece of waxed paper and trace your heart template onto it. Cut it out to create a mask for the "window" on the finished jar (fig. 2).

3. Place your heart sticker onto the jar front. Press firmly to get a good seal around all edges. Paint several layers of chalk paint onto the mason jar (fig. 3). Wait about 15 minutes between coats. Do not paint the bottom of the jar or the top lip of the jar. Paint away from the heart edges so that paint is not forced under the edge. Let dry.

4. Carefully peel the heart mask away from the jar, revealing your window (fig. 4). You may have some paint that bled under the edges. That's okay!

5. Use a toothpick to scrape away any noticeable messy edges around the heart (fig. 5).

Fig. 1: Cut a paper heart template.

Fig. 2: Trace a heart onto the masking tape.

Fig. 3: Cut out the tape heart. Stick it to the jar and paint.

Fig. 4: Peel away the mask.

Fig. 5: Clean up the paint edges.

Fig. 6: Add the glitter paint border.

Fig. 7: Trace the lid.

Fig. 8: Draw and cut the coin slot.

6. Place a dotted border of glitter puffy paint along the border of the heart window (fig. 6). Practice on paper a few times first to get a feel for the flow of paint.

7. Trace the flat disc portion of the mason jar lid onto scrap cardboard (fig. 7).

8. Use scissors to cut out the disc. Draw a thick line in the center of the disc to mark for the slot. Use your scissor points to make a hole in the center of the disc, and then cut carefully to create the coin slot (fig. 8). Then assemble the jar!

Crafting with Kindness 141

ACKNOWLEDGMENTS

I'd like to thank the team at Quarry, especially Joy, Marissa, Jessi, and the design team, who were terrific throughout.

I would like to thank my family, who helped me with photo setups when I needed extra hands. I'd also like to thank my dear friend Randi, who pitched in during the last few weeks when I was finishing up. I couldn't have made it down the home stretch without her!

ABOUT THE AUTHOR

Stephanie Corfee is an artist from the Philadelphia, Pennsylvania, area. She works from a home studio while also caring for her three sons and baby girl. "They all love to be in the studio with me. It's an inspiring place full of great light, colors, textures, and endless art supplies. Working in there is magic."

Stephanie's love for making art with kids is evident even in her personal work, which is full of whimsy and playful color. She works predominantly in acrylics and watercolor. Pencil sketches and ink doodles are also favorites. Her work is licensed and printed on wall art and greeting cards, plus products like bedding, scarves, totes, collectibles, and more.

Stephanie offers online workshops through her website, stephaniecorfee.com, and skillshare.com and is the author/illustrator of several art instructional books. *Craft Lab for Kids* is her sixth effort, and a seventh book is in the pipeline. "Teaching kids, whether in books, in person, or online, is just what I love to do. Helping kids gain confidence in their uniqueness and style is what inspires me most. It's one of the best feelings in the world."

INDEX

This book is for Coop, Grey, Lang & Ayla. My creativity and best ideas always start with you.

Brimming with creative inspiration, how-to projects, and useful information to enrich your everyday life, Quarto Knows is a favorite destination for those pursuing their interests and passions. Visit our site and dig deeper with our books into your area of interest: Quarto Creates, Quarto Cooks, Quarto Homes, Quarto Lives, Quarto Drives, Quarto Explores, Quarto Gifts, or Quarto Kids.

Text and Projects © 2020 Stephanie Corfee
Concept, Photography, and Presentation © 2020 Quarto Publishing Group USA Inc.

First Published in 2020 by Quarry Books, an imprint of The Quarto Group,
100 Cummings Center, Suite 265-D, Beverly, MA 01915, USA.
T (978) 282-9590 F (978) 283-2742 QuartoKnows.com

Quarry Books titles are also available at discount for retail, wholesale, promotional, and bulk purchase. For details, contact the Special Sales Manager by email at specialsales@quarto.com or by mail at The Quarto Group, Attn: Special Sales Manager, 100 Cummings Center, Suite 265-D, Beverly, MA 01915, USA.

10 9 8 7 6 5 4 3 2 1

ISBN: 978-1-63159-861-6

Digital edition published in 2020
eISBN: 978-1-63159-862-3

Library of Congress Cataloging-in-Publication Data

Names: Corfee, Stephanie, 1974- author.
Title: Craft lab for kids : 52 accessible projects to inspire, excite, and enable kids to create useful, beautiful handmade goods / Stephanie Corfee.
Description: Beverly, MA : Quarry Books, an imprint of The Quarto Group, 2020. | Series: Lab for kids | Includes index.
Identifiers: LCCN 2019051175 (print) | LCCN 2019051176 (ebook) | ISBN 9781631598616 (trade paperback) | ISBN 9781631598623 (ebook)
Subjects: LCSH: Handicraft for children.
Classification: LCC TT160 .C6757 2020 (print) | LCC TT160 (ebook) | DDC 745.5083--dc23
LC record available at https://lccn.loc.gov/2019051175
LC ebook record available at https://lccn.loc.gov/2019051176

Design: Debbie Berne
Page Layout: Megan Jones Design
Photography: Stephanie Corfee
Illustration: Shutterstock

Printed in China